MW00353246

SECULAR JUDAISM

To Felix Posen
Visionary, colleague and friend
for making it all possible

SECULAR JUDAISM
Faith, Values, and Spirituality

YAAKOV MALKIN
Tel Aviv University

Foreword by
RABBI SHERWIN T. WINE

VALLENTINE MITCHELL
LONDON • PORTLAND, OR

Published in 2004 in Great Britain by
VALLENTINE MITCHELL
Crown House, 47 Chase Side
Southgate, London N14 5BP

and in the United States of America by
VALLENTINE MITCHELL
c/o ISBS, 920 N. E. 58th Avenue, Suite 300
Portland, Oregon 97213-3786

Website: www.vmbooks.com

British Library Cataloguing in Publication Data

Malkin, Yaakov
Secular Judaism: Faith, Values, and Spirituality
1. Humanistic Judaism 2. Secularism 3. Faith (Judaism)
4. Jews – Identity
I. Title
296.8'34

ISBN 0-85303-513-X (paper)
ISBN 0-85303-512-1 (cloth)

Library of Congress Cataloging-in-Publication Data

Malkin, Yaakov, 1926–
Secular Judaism: Faith, Values, and Spirituality / Yaakov Malkin; foreword by Sherwin T. Wine.
p. cm.
Includes index.
ISBN 0-85303-512-1 (cloth) – ISBN 0-85303-513-X (pbk.)
I. Humanistic Judaism. 2. Secularism. 3. Religious pluralism–Judaism. 4. Spiritual life–Judaism. I. Title.

BM197.8.M36 2003
296.8'34–dc22

2003062165

Translated by Shmuel Gertel, Natalie Mendelson and Nachum Steigman.
Glossary by Nachum Steigman.
Cover design Ikan Mass Media
Painting (detail) Felice Pazner Malkin

Typeset in 10.5/13pt Palatino by Frank Cass Publishers
Printed in Great Britain by MPG Books Ltd, Bodmin, Cornwall

CONTENTS

FOREWORD

This book is an important book. It provides an intellectual and philosophical foundation for a new movement in Jewish life. Secular Humanistic Judaism was created to serve the needs, both in Israel and the Diaspora, of secular Jews who want their Jewish identity to have depth and significance. Yaakov Malkin is one of the significant intellectual leaders of this movement. Although he is an Israeli, his book speaks very directly to the secular Jews of North America and the English-speaking world.

In North America the question of Jewish identity was for a long time in the hands of the Reform movement. America was this strange place in the nineteenth century where the Jewish establishment was not Orthodox but Reform. When the Reform movement first emerged in Europe, the Jews were struggling with the twin intrusions of both the Enlightenment and the Emancipation. The offer of national citizenship to the Jews was both wonderful and troubling. Since their beginnings the Jews had functioned as a nation. Even when their government became a theocracy and religious conformity was enforced, they still saw themselves as primarily a nation. Even when they became a world people in the Diaspora, they still saw themselves as a nation. In the Middle Ages the Jews were never regarded as members of the nations among whom they lived. They saw themselves and were viewed by others as aliens. Even their ambitions reflected this sense of alienation. They were consumed by Messianic practices that promised to return them to their historic homeland.

National identity for Jews as French, German and English was, therefore, problematic. Can a person be a member of two nations simultaneously? If you join a new nation must you repudiate the nation from which you came? Or, if you are pious and loyal to your ancestral past, do you repudiate the offer of citizenship that is extended? The ultra-Orthodox rejectionists, in their pious consistency, chose to refuse the offer. But almost all Jews accepted. Their acceptance preserved the dilemma. Almost from the beginning of emancipation, the enemies of the Jews accused them of dual loyalty. To counter this accusation, the leaders of Reform, who favored cultural assimilation, resolved the dilemma. They proclaimed that Jewish identity was only a religious identity, that Judaism was only a religion – and that German Jews were only patriotic Germans of the Mosaic persuasion.

The German Reformers brought this new sense of Jewish identity to America. American Jews, according to them, were Jews only by virtue of religion. If Mr. Cohen decided to become an Episcopalian he ceased to be Jewish. If Mr. Lipshiptz discovered he was an atheist, he stopped being Jewish at the very instant he stopped believing in God. The word "Jewish" no longer had any ethnic or national content. It was a purely voluntary identity akin to Christian identity. The heart of Judaism was theological belief. To understand Judaism was to understand that its essence was monotheistic. The Bible was not Jewish literature. It was holy scripture, the message of one God to the world through the Jewish prophets. The Jews, as patriotic Americans, were no different from the Methodists or Presbyterians except in theological matters. In three decades we were transformed into a religious denomination.

Of course, the triumph of Reform, in America, coincided with the rise of the new anti-semitism in Europe. For the anti-semites the Jews were a nation or "race" as they used the word in the nineteenth century. Jewish identity was involuntary. Jewish assimilation was impossible. Jewish culture was incompatible with Western culture. Anti-semitism was troubling for Reform Jews, not only because of the perceived danger but also because it refused to recognize the Jews as only a religious denomination.

When Eastern European Jews arrived in North America, the Reformers were appalled by the image they projected. It was not only their poverty and immigrant crudeness that bothered them. It was the fact that they were a distinct nationality, with a language and culture all their own. Russian Jews did not think that they were Russian. They saw themselves as ethnically Jewish. Yiddish, not Russian, was their mother tongue. Their self-image was that of a nation. The counterpart to "Jew" was not so much "Christian" as it was "Italian" or "Irish." The very presence of these Eastern Jews was an indictment of the stand that Reform had taken on Jewish identity. But, strangely enough, in the hinterlands of America the Reform definition persisted.

Even the arrival of Zionism, Hitler and the Holocaust did not overthrow this absurd religious self-definition. Many Reform leaders devoted their lives to fighting Zionism, because the perception of the Jews as a nation and of Judaism as a national culture was anathema to them. The Holocaust and the establishment of the state of Israel destroyed the opposition to Zionism; but it did not eliminate the perception of Jewish identity that the old Reformers had presented. For most official occasions, especially if Christians were present, the Jews were featured only as a theological fraternity. Why a theological fraternity would need a national homeland must have puzzled the audience.

Now, a religious definition of Jewish identity means that there can be no secular Jews. According to the old Reformers, once you become secular you cease to be Jewish. But this assertion was clearly absurd. There were thousands of self-proclaimed secular Jews. Some of them were involved in Yiddishist and Zionist schools and organizations. Some of them were socialists. Some of them were capitalists. But all of them were clearly Jewish in the eyes of both Jews and non-Jews. Nevertheless, secular Jews in America were always made to feel that they were less Jewish because they were not religious. The rabbis were clearly the spokespersons for Judaism. When Judaism was discussed, a Reform, Conservative or modern Orthodox rabbi would be standing there to describe what Judaism was all about. But no secular Jew was ever invited to do that at any official occasion of the Jewish community. Unorganized, dis-spirited and peripheral, the secular Jew often saw himself as a second-class citizen in the Jewish community.

What North American Jews needed was an ideology about Judaism that would rescue them from this religious "monopoly;" an ideology that could be turned into communities, congregations, schools, teachers, leaders and literature.

The foundation of this "revival" lay in the work of two Jewish intellectuals who sought to transform the meaning of Judaism. The first was the Russian Jewish historian Simon Dubnow. The second was the Zionist ideologue Asher Ginsberg, who took the name of Ahad Ha-am. Both of them did not wish to leave the word "Judaism" in the hands of the religious, whether Reform or Orthodox. Both of them wanted to build on the historic national identity of Jewish self-consciousness. (In the Diaspora "Jewish

People" is a more comfortable designation than "Jewish nation.") For both Dubnow and Ahad Ha-am Judaism included religion for those who were religious. But it was broader than that. "Judaism" was analogous to the word "Hellenism." Just as Hellenism was the historic culture of the Greek people, so was Judaism the historic culture of the Jewish People. Culture includes much more than religion. Culture includes language, literature, music, dance, food and celebration. Culture includes secular Jews because all cultures feature many opposing ideologies. No single ideology or philosophy defines Judaism. It embraces them all in the broad arms of a cultural self-image.

Mordecai Kaplan, the father of Reconstructionist Judaism, was deeply influenced by Ahad Ha-am. He used this definition and added the word "civilization" to the word "culture." But he betrayed his mentor by insisting that the culture was inseparable from religion and religious vocabulary.

Secular Humanistic Judaism regards itself as the heir of Simon Dubnow and Ahad Ha-am. It affirms unequivocally that Judaism is more than just a religion, that Judaism is a culture of the Jewish people, embracing within its fold the religious and the secular, the theist and the atheist, the capitalist and the socialist, the traditionalist and the radical – all united pluralistically in the enjoyment of its riches. For secular Jews, Judaism as a culture means full participation in the life of the Jewish people.

But the big question remains. If Judaism is culture and I am a cultural Jew, how do I lead my life as a Jew, especially as a Jew in the Diaspora? What do I read? What do I study? What do I celebrate? How do I celebrate? How do I connect my culture to my ethical values and my ethical action? What do I do to use my culture for personal inspiration and spiritual enrichment?

The best articulator of Judaism as a culture is Yaakov Malkin. If you want answers to these questions, read this book.

Rabbi Sherwin T. Wine, Dean
International Institute for Secular Humanistic Jews
Farmington Hills, Michigan, USA

INTRODUCTION

WHAT DO SECULAR HUMANIST JEWS BELIEVE?

The past two hundred years have seen a remarkable shift of the role of religion in defining the core identity of both Jewry (the collective defined as Jews) and Judaism (the spiritual and cultural conceptual framework of that identity). The emergence of civic ideologies, the principle of separation between religion and state and the development of secular Judaism have all created a new agenda for collective Jewish identity.

The new agenda is not only a call for liberation from religion, a "lack of belief." It is also a recognition of the need to integrate humanistic principles and Jewish culture based on belief. Religion has no monopoly over the concept of belief. What I propose to do in this book is spell out the beliefs that secular lifestyles both declare and imply. I will attempt to define what the majority of secular Jews believe in.

The book is both descriptive and ascriptive, observing the lived reality of most secular Jews and articulating principles and directions for secular Jewry. There will be a strong emphasis on Israel, with significant implications for Judaism in general. The first reason for this is historical: modern secular Judaism expressed itself as part of the world culture and, primarily, as a part of the mostly secular Zionist movement, a movement born to oppose the religious ideology of Diaspora and "exile." Aside from Zionism, there were other approaches to secular Judaism. They died (or, more precisely, were murdered) in the Shoah. The second reason for the emphasis on Israel is simply the fact that it is home to a substantial number of the world's Jews, who live within a full spectrum of a national, religious and secular Jewish environment.

Secular beliefs stress freedom over commandments, and they are shared by the majority of Jews, both within Israel and around the world. These beliefs are rarely examined in a systematic way, and I hope to do so here. The introduction sets out a general framework of principles for considering the question, "What do secular Jews believe?" Chapter 1 discusses the role of humanistic values and their general purpose – to innovate. Chapter 2 develops the pluralistic, historical approach to Judaism and advances the concept of Judaism as culture. It examines the relationship between the two defining frameworks of Judaism, a religion and a "nation," and discusses the relationship of Judaism to democratic values. Chapter 3 raises the inevitable question, "Who is a Jew?" and points to the Bible as the source of Jewish collective memory and the foundation of Jewish civilization and culture. It explores the role of secular Zionism in the transformation of Jewish history, as well as the relationships between Israeli and Jewish identities. Chapter 4 looks at the legacy of Judaism's foundational texts and the relationship of secular Jews to God as a "literary hero" who functions in the collective reality and history of Judaism. Chapter 5 claims that the desire for pluralism in Judaism is in accord with authentic and ancient Jewish life and tradition, such as that of the Talmudic era. It also points to the ancient mechanism of debate, with its implied democratic values, and the significance of temporally limited majority decisions that leave the door open for future change and adaptation. Chapter 6 addresses a major issue confronting Western, liberal democracies: the confusion between pluralism and relativism. In the name of the latter, democracies (Israel included) have permitted the establishment of organizations and political parties that deny the validity of the democratic process and draw their authority from outside the framework of state and society. Relativism is also discussed as a moral danger, as it inevitably leads to dehumanization. Chapter 7 provides a secular, humanistic and pluralistic perspective on the need for spirituality. Drawing on Martin Buber's "I and Thou" concept, it examines the search for the sublime and emphasizes the community and its principles of education. Chapter 8 takes on the issue of education, proposing a new orientation and a set of guiding principles for a curriculum that applies the concept of Judaism as culture. It draws on theoretical issues, as well as on the practical experience of secular communities and Israeli institutions of higher learning.

Jews who have liberated themselves from the prohibitions and coercion of the *Halakhic* (see Glossary) religion, the people called "secular" or "freethinkers," are in fact believing Jews, but not in the orthodox sense. Secular humanist Jews live according to their beliefs, and they judge themselves and others by the humanist values that constitute these beliefs. Humanists believe that men and women created God, not the other way around. While they acknowledge that God is central to the Bible, a foundational religious text, Jewish humanists believe that the values of humanism are compatible with what they see as Judaism. And they believe in the right to choose for themselves how to realize their Jewishness.

Values are the yardsticks men and women fashion to judge and rank any commandment (or *mitzva*), law, regime or form of behaviour. Secular values and beliefs, like religious ones, declare themselves in lifestyles, in the education we choose for our children, in the ceremonies we choose for our festivals and in our political behavior.

Jewish religious tradition does not recognize any obligatory credo. Jewish beliefs are expressed in the way Jews live their lives, celebrate the religious-historical festivals, mark the turning points of birth, marriage and death, and observe (or choose not to observe) the *mitzvot*. Practice and belief together place Jews in one of contemporary Jewry's many "Judaisms" – Secular, Orthodox, Reform, Conservative and Reconstructionist, among others.

Some beliefs are declared in new forms of ceremony and celebration.

A "freethinking" trend that may be traced back to Maimonides and that has metamorphosed Jewry in the past two hundred years has brought about a search for new "rites of passage" (to mark births, marriages, deaths etc.) and for new ways to mark the seasonal festivals. The Israeli experience is illuminating. Hundreds of contemporary Passover *Haggadahs*, for example, have been composed and published in an attempt to give new face and form to the great Exodus festival and break the mold in which Rabbi Amram and Rabbi Saadiah cast the *Haggadah* in the ninth and tenth centuries. For other festivals as well, the rabbinically determined traditional form of celebration has lost meaning for freethinkers, who continue to search for new form and content. The Hanukkah festival, honoring the Maccabean victory against an attempt to rob the Jewish people of its religion and civilization, is another example. Rabbinical interpretation deleted the Maccabees and their history (related in the four Books of the Maccabees) from the festival, commemorating instead the miracle of the holy oil. Freethinking Judaism has restored the Books of Maccabees to their rightful place in the evolution of Judaism and has also reinstated the original purpose of Hanukkah – to commemorate the people's fight for its cultural and religious freedom.

Other beliefs are declared in political behavior and culture. The fact that the majority of Israel's electorate participate in and demonstrate support for the country's secular democracy attests to its preference over the rule of *Halakha* and obedience to rabbis who claim to draw their authority directly from the divine. The majority of citizens support democracy's core principles and institutions, which should be upheld, they believe, by the rule of law, the separation of powers, and a constitution that defends the rights of individuals and determines their obligations to society. This is the political culture that most Israelis desire and defend; it is also the framework that assigns *Halakha* its proper place in their lives. Although such values may appear self-evident for citizens of Western democracies, this is not the case in Israel, where most religious parties would like to implement the *Halakha* as state law. When most Israeli Jews vote for political parties organized along democratic lines and not controlled by (mostly non-elected) rabbis, they are demonstrating their belief in human sovereignty and the right of men and women to manage their own lives and pursue humanist values, the sole guarantors of a free society.

Beliefs are also declared in education systems. Since we are at a point in history where nearly every society is a national society, secular Jews believe they have a vital bond to the national culture they have inherited. Since no people lives in isolation and no national culture is unconnected to a universal, human culture, they believe it equally vital to maintain an open line to non-Jewish societies and cultures. This openness is reflected in most Israeli education systems, and it is paralleled by the openness in the country's mass media and literature, its scholarship and arts, its vernacular on the streets and its approach to the Bible and the other sources of Judaism.

The character of religious Jewish school systems and yeshivas (religious college seminaries) and the sort of material they teach (and have always taught) reflects the belief systems held by only a portion of Jewry's many Judaisms. Today, the large majority of Israeli parents send their children to non-religious schools, and the same is true in the Diaspora. The size of this majority, compared with the much smaller minority of parents who send their children to religious schools and yeshivas, parallels the ratio of the non-religious to the *Halakhically* observant in world Jewry today. Parents who choose not to send their children to a religious school are conveying their preference for education that exposes its students to the wider Jewish culture and stimulates them to take a critical view of all of human products and achievements, among them the sources of Judaism. These parents are demonstrating their faith in education that equips students to assess, and then to accept or disown, any commandment, law or custom, and provides them with the necessary skills for living in the modern world.

Secular humanist Jews believe in universal moral values, values that pass a rational test: to what degree, if at all, do they enable and stimulate human beings to achieve their potential humanity and enjoy a good quality of life? To secular humanist Jews, this test produces unequivocal results in favor of laws that embody universal moral values, as opposed to religious commandments (*mitzvot*), which do not. It is their conviction that the ultimate purpose of all values and laws is to promote the good of humanity and the quality of life, and not to strive for compatibility with laws that come from God or from *Halakhic* "authorities."

It is through such convictions that secular Jews have liberated themselves from all obligation of obedience to commandments that fail the "achieving humanity" test. They will disqualify, for instance, any *Halakha* that oppresses women or any *mitzva* that has lost all meaning for them, such as ritual prayers to a God whom they believe humans themselves have created. For secular Jews, a liberal democracy is paramount for them as Jews and as human beings. A democratic society guarantees its citizens the rights to equality and liberty, hence the right to be free of the *Halakhic* code and any undemocratic legislation passed to impose that code on those who do not adhere to it.

As we shall see, secular, pluralistic humanism recognizes that its values have been embedded in Judaism for centuries. This understanding is integral to the concept of Judaism as culture developed in this book, as a paradigm for interpreting the place of secular Judaism today and as a starting point for setting a future agenda.

CHAPTER 1

WHO IS A JEW? JEWISH IDENTITIES AND THEIR DIFFERENCES

Membership in the Jewish People can be the result of birth into a Jewish family, religious conversion or voluntary enlistment by one of the numerous methods used from Biblical times to our own. The various types of formal religious conversion today are merely among the many routes by which non-Jews have been made Jews. The most common is marriage, the route taken by Ruth the Moabite.

Every human being belongs to a social, ethnic or other form of national culture. There is no one who is not a member of some national entity, as defined by language, culture, a known historical heritage, education or custom. "Jewishness" is recognized today as a belonging to a people, the nationality of Jews, and its defining elements are all or some of the following:

- Birth into a Jewish family or joining a Jewish family or community by any method.
- Formal conversion to the Jewish religion through the method used by one of Jewry's religious denominations.
- Membership in a Jewish community or society, religious or secular.
- Education and rearing in a Jewish culture, religious or secular.
- Awareness of the Jews' common historical-cultural legacy.
- Acknowledgement of the Bible as the foundation of all Jewry's "Judaisms."
- Acknowledgement of Hebrew as the Jews' ancient/modern national language.
- Knowledge of one of the languages spoken only by Jews (such as Yiddish, Ladino, Tatai, Moghrabi), and some knowledge of that language's culture.
- Acknowledgement of the Land of Israel as the Jews' ancient homeland.

THE JEWS: A UNIQUE PEOPLE

Every national entity is unique, for what defines it as a people – its qualities and its place among other peoples and cultures – is peculiar to itself. What defines and distinguishes the Swiss, as a nation, is quite different from what defines and distinguishes the Swedes, the Zulu, the Inuit and the Jews. No single definition of "people" suits them all. The defining qualities of Jews are their common national history and their capacity to embrace divergent and contradictory beliefs.

"Territory" is not the defining quality of a nation. There are peoples, like the Kurds, dispersed across several nations and having none of their own. Conversely, there are cases of many peoples living in one territory under one national label, as is the case in Nigeria, China, Canada and Belgium. Some peoples – the Gypsies, the Bedouin – have no settled land base at all.

Ever since they settled in Canaan, the Jews have had one homeland. In ancient times, it was divided into two Jewish states that had alternately fraternal and hostile relations. Then, for some two thousand years, they lived in and were expelled from dozens of lands and states, without having a state of their own. In our own time, they returned to and resettled what they had never stopped calling their homeland, a land they now shared with another people, just as they had in the ancient past.

Social scientists, ever trying to build unitary definitions, have found it very hard to reconcile themselves to the fact that no one people is like another. During the centuries when the Jews lived scattered across a huge Diaspora, without a single common spoken language, they were generally denied the status of a people. Then, scholars came to understand that what makes a group a people (or an "ethnic entity") is different for each one, no less than the history that sets the group apart from every other.

No individual can be defined as a person merely by stating the qualities he or she shares with others, and neither can a people. For example, having said that someone is clever, generous, bad-hearted or silly, we still have a long way to go to describe his or her singularity. With no individual biography, we cannot characterize a person, and the same is true for peoples: each people has its biography defined by one or more of the historical factors that went into shaping its unique national culture. Among these we may number:

- its shared historical experience
- its sense of, and bonding to, a historical-cultural heritage
- a dominant spoken and written language or languages
- its interrelationships with other peoples, past and present
- a unifying – or divisive – religious cult or cults
- the evolution of its religion and secularization
- works of art and scholarship, which both the people and outsiders regard as embodiments of the national culture
- lifestyles, festivals and rites shared by most of the people.

In every period of history all or some of these things have contributed to molding Jewish self-consciousness and sense of identity. Predominant among them – at all times – has been the conviction that all Jews share a single historical-cultural heritage. Their diversity of opinion and belief about religious faith, *mitzva* observance, the existence, nature and exclusivity of God, nationality, messianism, Zionism and the gentiles – though all this may have been no less than kaleidoscopic, nothing has ever shaken that basic certainty about their historical heritage.

Other religious cultures – Catholic, Shi'ite, Protestant, Buddhist – have projected one faith and cult over a number of peoples and nations, each one retaining its own sense of collective identity, nationality, and historical-cultural biography. Italians, Irish, Poles, Mexicans and Timorese, for example, share the Catholic conception of God and worship. The Jews, by contrast, created a unique fusion of religion and nationality. However, it was a fusion that sustained national unity only by accommodating a turbulent pluralism in approaches to "religion," "faith" and "nationality." Within that Jewish nationhood, separate "ethnic" and cultural identities formed – Sephardi and Ashkenazi, American, French, Israeli, and many more.

THE BIBLE: COLLECTIVE MEMORY AND THE FOUNDATION OF JEWISH CIVILIZATION AND CULTURE

The story of the Jewish People, as told in the books of the Bible, has become Jewry's collective memory, as potent now as ever. The heart of the Jewish people's collective sense of identity and nationhood is the Bible (the Old Testament), a fact acknowledged equally by Jews and others.

The Bible is an anthology of historical chronicles, codes of law, and literary works (and much more), composed during the first fifteen hundred years of the Jews' existence as a people. There is no proof that its chronicles reflect precise events. In the collective historical memory, however, they have become "historical truths," as perceived by Ahad Ha'am – that is, truths that act on and in Jewish history, spiritual-cultural life and the workings of state and society with the power and authority of proven fact.

Whether, as some believe, the books of the Bible reflect a historical record, its internal contradictions and variant accounts notwithstanding, the people's collective memory acknowledges a single national tradition founded in the Bible. The saga begins, as most Jews see it, in the nomadic wanderings of a few extended families of Hebrews, who joined together as a tribal coalition, the "Children of Israel," and liberated themselves from slavery in Egypt, wandered the desert, settled in Canaan, and coalesced into two Israelite kingdoms. Several hundred years later, both kingdoms ended in destruction. The surviving leaders and elite were taken into exile in Mesopotamia, where they built a new society and community; in time, a small portion of them returned to Judaea.

Each of these stages in the narrative of the Jewish People is recounted in the 39 books of the Bible. The same books also describe the people's legal, social, political, military and religious institutions, its multiple religious divisions ("pluralism" from a different, more positive, point of view) and certain famous works of art, including those in the three great temples erected to Yahweh in the two pre-exilic kingdoms.

Secular and religious Jews alike share this collective memory – and it is still potent. The divergent conclusions drawn from the biblical narratives regarding the Jews' right to the Land of Israel, or the rightful borders of the state, still fuel modern Israeli national politics.

Every time Jews welcome in the Sabbath or celebrate one of the national festivals and holy days, these historical narratives are replayed. All Jewry's denominations recognize that this ancient anthology, the Bible, is the source of their Judaism and the common reference for so much of what was later written and created. This is as true of secular Jewry as it is of Jewry's observant sectors – Reform, Conservative and Orthodox. Even the ultra-Orthodox minority sects, for whom studying Judaism means studying Talmud and Midrash and nothing more, acknowledge the Bible as their common basis.

The role of the Bible in Jewish collective memory is much more evident in Israel than it is in the Diaspora, thanks to its very prominent place in the Israeli state (secular) school curriculum. The Hebrew that schoolchildren write and speak originates in the Bible, and it displays its origin in everyday discourse. Archaeological discoveries and the public debate over exactly what land belongs to "the Land of Israel" also keep the Bible alive and relevant to every Israeli. The more Diaspora Jews are familiar with the Bible and the culture and civilization rooted in it, the more they will share in a worldwide national Jewish identity. The reverse, unfortunately, is equally true.

The Bible may be the one constituent of Judaism on which every Jewish denomination, sect and movement has founded its culture. However, through centuries of slanted teaching, understanding of that foundation has been influenced by just one of these movements – Orthodoxy. Most Jews hardly remember the extent to which the Bible chronicles pluralism. For example, it offers multiple versions of the Creation and of David's life story, and many other events are recounted from two viewpoints. For the most part, the multiple currents in Israelite religious life, such as the conflict between pagan polytheism and Yahwist monotheism, are readily apparent.

The non-biblical sources of the Jewish collective memory are controversial in a different way. The Books of the Maccabees and histories written by famous Hellenizing Jews (such as Josephus, Philo of Alexandria, Jason of Cyrenaica and others) were well respected in the Greek- and Latin-speaking Jewish Diasporas until the rabbis "excommunicated" them from Jewish society and culture. It took the freethinkers to restore these texts to their deserved status in Judaism, one that the ultra-Orthodox still refuse to acknowledge.

The discoveries and re-evaluations of biblical archaeologists are also ignored by the ultra-Orthodox. The Bible alone, respected and honored by every sector of Jewry, is still considered the only source of authority by the ultra-Orthodox.

SECULAR ZIONISM AND THE TRANSFORMATION OF JEWISH HISTORY

The realization of the Zionist vision in the State of Israel is secular Jewry's greatest historical achievement. The greater part of religious Jewry had opposed Zionism, convinced that Jews were duty-bound to sit patiently in exile and wait for Yahweh's messiah. Hostility was also expressed by other secular movements, which believed that the nationalist, territorial solution to the Jews' problems was wrong-headed.

Only small groups of religious Jews, some Zionist and some anti-Zionist, some messianic and some anti-messianic, joined the majority secular group in Palestine starting at the end of the nineteenth century. Larger numbers came later when many Jewish communities were forced to flee their host countries. Though most of these were Jews who regarded themselves as "traditional," in practice they led a secular way of life.

Zionism is Jewry's national liberation movement. However, the dramatic transition from the status of a persecuted/tolerated minority to a sovereign people in its own homeland went beyond the issue of territory. Social structures and lifestyles changed, and the ancient national language was restored from a near-defunct vehicle of prayer and esoteric literature to a spoken mass vernacular. Secular Zionism created a new, autonomous society with all its necessary institutions, from an educational system to a parliament – and free of rabbinical authority. Decades later, this process of sociopolitical construction culminated in the founding of a democratic nation-state. In all this, the chief movers were the secular Zionists. They committed themselves to resettling the homeland and made good on their commitment, with help and encouragement from supporters in the Diaspora.

By the end of the twentieth century, more than half the world's Jews under 18 years old lived in Israel. Twenty years from now, the majority of all Jews in the world will be Israelis.

The driving force of Zionism was the conviction that Jews had waited long enough for God's messiah; it was time they took redemption into their own hands. The State of Israel is the fruit of that conviction. Hardly had its establishment been declared when it proved itself by enabling Jews, for the first time since the Hasmoneans (some 2,200 years earlier), to defeat military forces sent to destroy them.

Israel's military victories and successes in building its economy and society led to its gradual recognition, by world Jewry and the world's nations, as the centre of the Jewish world and the flagship of the Jewish People. It was not until the victorious Six-Day War proved that Israel was not going to be wiped off the map that certain Jewish pacifist intellectual circles came to the same recognition.

Today, the Jewish State maintains its Zionist function. Residence and citizenship is granted to every Jew who arrives either by choice or as a refugee. This is the essence and main purpose of Zionism and is no less than a redefinition of the rights of Jews the world over. Israel as a place of "asylum" was most evident at the time of the Nazis' "Final Solution," when Jews were refused entry by almost every nation, however "enlightened."

A NEW SECULAR ISRAELI CULTURE AND A DIFFERENT TYPE OF JEWISH SOCIETY

The first secular cooperative communities were settled in Palestine early in the twentieth century. They were the *kibbutzim* and *moshavim,* invented and built to farm the land (the former cooperatively organized, the latter semi-cooperative). Other types of secular communities were the *khavurot* (groups that met regularly for Jewish sociocultural activities outside the synagogue framework) and the "cultural communities" centered on a *bet ha'am* (a building designed as the centre for wide-ranging, year-round social, cultural and intellectual activities). These secular communities also cultivated new cultural institutions, new rites and traditions, new ways of celebrating the festivals. Though some of their outward forms and ideas may have borrowed liberally from Judaism's religious heritage and the Bible, the core of the communities was their secular vision of the world.

These communities of secular Jews welcomed the Sabbath, celebrated major seasonal holidays, and marked the turning points of the human lifecycle. The time-venerated schedule of prayer and religious ritual was jettisoned, however, replaced by symbols of the new culture. To commemorate special occasions, songs, verses, stories, speeches and sayings were composed or adapted from contemporary culture. New images were institutionalized: carrying in the first fruits of the harvest on *Shavuot* (Pentecost); planting trees on *Tu B'Shvat* (the New Year for Trees); reshaping the Passover *Seder* in accordance with newly composed *Haggadahs;* mounting *Adloyada* (carnival) processions that changed the face of Purim. Days of Remembrance were inserted into the calendar to commemorate the Holocaust, Israel's independence and its defensive wars. New ways were found to conduct weddings, bar- and bat-mitzvah ceremonies and funerals.

The thousands of pages of text and descriptions of festival rites now stored in the secular festival archives at Kibbutz Bet Hashita and Kibbutz Ramat Yohanan (and elsewhere) are witness to the intensive creative efforts poured into fashioning this new secular culture. Within a few years, the thousands of new songs composed and the hundreds of new dances choreographed had become the "folk songs" and "folk dances" of the new secular Jewry. Festivals of song and dance were organized, and Israeli dance groups began touring internationally, demonstrating Israel's "folk-dance tradition."

Literature, theater, the plastic and performing arts, philosophy and scholarship did not lag far behind. New works found audiences in freethinking communities around the world; even observant Reform, Conservative and Reconstructionist congregations began incorporating the work of secular Israelis into their synagogue services and school syllabi. Even more receptive were the secular synagogue congregations and *khavurot*, both of which began multiplying in America and Europe in the last quarter of the twentieth century. By the end of the century, Israeli Jewish writing, theatre, cinema and music had become known worldwide, creating a new image for Jewish culture and civilization. Secular Israeli authors, whose works were translated from the Hebrew original, won renown as representatives of a new Jewish culture.

ISRAELI-NESS AND JEWISHNESS

As we have seen, the national identity of Jewishness is the result of either birth or joining the Jewish People in one of many possible ways. What is new about Jewish cultural identity in Israel? Among all possible Jewish identities, the Israeli-Jewish one is unique in that only in Israel are Jewish children raised and educated in the context of one historical-cultural heritage, a Jewish national culture and a common Jewish language.

While Israeli culture, like all cultures, is suffused with intrusions and borrowings from other peoples, the education system is Jewish (the Arab-Israeli curriculum is autonomous) and teaches students their Judaism in vernacular, modern Hebrew.

The secular Israeli-Jewish identity of the majority of the Jewish population is still in the process of formation and development, emerging from the new Hebrew culture and the legacy of the

Jewish-ethnic-immigrant cultures brought over from five continents. It is a secularism that often has fruitful contact with the culture of "traditional" (*masorti*) Jewish society. But between this secular-traditional society and the society of the Orthodox (and those close to them) the gap is widening. The secular and the Orthodox (especially the ultra-Orthodox) differ in almost every way imaginable: their styles of dress, the languages they speak and/or understand, the arts and communications media to which they are exposed and their attitudes and positions regarding the army, democracy, courts of law, the parliament, basic humanist values of equality and freedom, human rights, the perception of Jewish history, the Bible and other canonical texts, the *Halakha*, and non-Jews and non-Orthodox Jews. In fact, the differences are rooted in the response to almost every component of contemporary Jewish and non-Jewish civilization.

Within the secular population, the process of "interethnic mixing" (Ashkenazi, Sephardi, etc.) and fusion is accelerating as the children and grandchildren of immigrants intermarry. This phenomenon has interesting implications for the articulation of Israeli culture in music, theatre, cinema and literature.

The second, third and fourth generations of secular Israelis generally accept the rich marketplace of immigrant cultures as a common heritage, and they freely engage in them. Among the ultra-Orthodox, however, interethnic mixing is strictly prohibited. Each sect and movement marries within itself and insists on its own schools, synagogues and communal institutions. The ultra-Orthodox try to maintain as wide and unbridgeable a gap as possible between Ashkenazi and Sephardi Jews.

CHAPTER 2

HUMANISM, NATIONALITY AND SECULAR JEWISH CULTURE

"Secular Judaism" is a term referring to the community of Jews who do not adhere to the *Halakhic* religious commandments (*mitzvot*). "Secular Judaism" is also a term referring to the culture and creations of the Jewish population free of adherence to *mitzvot*.

THE PRECEDENCE OF VALUES OVER COMMANDMENTS

The major issue over which secular and Orthodox Jews battle is one of precedence: the values of democracy and humanism on the one hand and the *mitzvot* of the *Halakhic* code on the other. This fundamental disagreement over precedence lies at the heart of the "culture war" now being fought between a majority convinced of the supremacy of democracy and an Orthodox minority, equally certain that *Halakha* has precedence over democracy and the laws of the civil state.

Compromise is not a possibility because both sides are dealing in absolute values. The secular belief in the fundamentals of humanism is backed by rational judgement. It is a position that non-religious children absorb from their first days at school. Belief in the supremacy of the *mitzvot*, on the other hand, draws its strength from the belief that these commandments are divine, inviolable and unalterable, to be obeyed if only out of fear of the Creator's judgment.

The priority of humanism over all other values has been encapsulated in three famous tenets: one of Hillel the Elder – "Do not do unto others what you would hate done to you;" and two of Immanuel Kant – "Each man is an end in his own right and may never be seen as a means to another's end" and "No rule is ethical which is not of universal application." Without these three rationally argued values there can be no humanity in human society. They stipulate that the ends of morality are the good of human beings, the quality of their lives, and the extent of their humanity. They affirm that women and men are the source of all authority and the authors of all values and laws, and hence they have the authority to alter values and laws, choose how they will be made and determine when their validity has lapsed.

This is not a position that has any bearing on the Orthodox faith, which contends that the exclusive source of authority is Yahweh, that all the *Halakhic mitzvot* were dictated by him to Moses on Mount Sinai, that only Orthodox rabbis enjoy the right to interpret them and that man-made laws have no power to nullify them.

This fundamental rupture has given rise to the disputes that currently beset Israel's secular and religious camps and is of vital interest to Jewish communities throughout the world.

The State of Israel has given priority to its humanism-based "Foundational Laws" (its constitution-in-the-making) over *mitvzot* and rabbinical laws. These "Foundational Laws" establish and protect human freedom and dignity, equal obligations by all citizens, freedom of employment and freedom of choice.

Some of these laws are still in the process of formation by the Knesset, the Israeli parliament. The key areas of conflict with religious law are the following:

Fully equal rights of men and women: The rights in question are in all spheres, including the courts, which preside over matters relating to marriage, divorce, and education. Rabbinical Courts exercising authority in these matters have decreed that women may be judged but cannot be judges.

The character and content of Jewish education: Will it teach Judaism and the history of Jewry in the context of world culture or as a closed, detached system? Will it prepare students for an active role in society and the economy or confine their knowledge to the Talmud? Will it equip students to make their own rational criticism of Judaism's sources and traditions or merely sanctify rabbinical tradition and exposition?

The Law of Return and conversion to Judaism: Will the Law of Return (giving all Jews arriving in Israel the right to Israeli residence and citizenship) apply to all who have joined the Jewish people in any way or only to the children of a Jewish mother? Will joining the Jewish people be made contingent on religious conversion in conformity with the *Halakhic* rulings of a single Jewish sect, or will other routes to Judaism be opened, as they were in Biblical times?

Official recognition for *all* denominations of Judaism and their leaders, secular or religious, as legitimate representatives of one of Jewry's many Judaisms: At present Israel subjects Reform and Conservative Jews and their rabbis, as well as other non-Orthodox Jews, to discrimination and disqualification.

Compulsory military conscription: Will conscription be made compulsory for all Israeli citizens or remain so only for the secular, with the religious entitled to exemption? In army units headed by an army officer *and* a rabbi (which include students from the Orthodox *yeshivot hesder*, a framework combining army service with Yeshiva studies), will soldiers obey the orders of the officer or the rabbi?

The imposition of the Sabbath and holy-day laws on secular Jews who want to celebrate their weekends and festivals in their own way: How can religion and state be separated so as to allow religious communities to go their own way, according to their own customs, but within the framework of the state's democratic laws and with the stipulation that they fulfil their obligations to the state no less than other citizens?

Each of these disputes has an impact on Israeli life, and in none can a solution be reached through compromise. They can be settled only through the democratic process ending in majority decisions that respect the rights of various groups within society. Certainly, there should be ongoing dialogue between the two sides to create as much mutual understanding as possible. It is best, however, that both sides acknowledge from the outset that neither compromise nor consensus will settle these conflicts.

Democracy is driven not only by majority decision but also by a commitment to the rights of minorities and individuals, and it is this quality that makes it the sole guarantor of peaceful coexistence between Jewry's diverse Judaisms. Given such coexistence, Jewish education systems – secular and religious – would each function autonomously and give full expression to the belief system and lifestyle of the parent community. A necessary corollary would have to be that each system fulfil minimum uniform curriculum requirements, as in the case of France.

Since the leaders of most religions do not view democracy favorably, it has been long recognized that it is vital for democracies to separate the powers of the state from the authority of religious establishments. All Western democracies have institutionalized this separation. In Israel, divorcing the institutions of Judaism, Christianity and Islam from those of the state will liberate religious leaders from the embarrassment of being salaried officials of a secular government and will also liberate the state's elected institutions from subservience to the dictates of non-elected religious authorities.

ACHIEVING OUR HUMANITY – SUPREME GOAL, SUPREME VALUE

Men and women grow into their humanity and absorb humanist values. The "human animal" is not automatically humane, but has to mature into its humanity and win the battle against dehumanization. Brought up by a pack of wolves, it will behave like a wolf. Given a racist education, there is a good chance it will be unable to distinguish good from evil.

Guided into its humanity, it will become humane. The end by which we judge and rank all values and laws is their contribution to making human beings humane. Man is not the measure of all things: man's humanity is a much better yardstick.

This very duality of potential – to become humane or inhumane – is what differentiates the human species from other animals. Every other animal has no choice but to fulfil the instructions of its genome. Only man is sufficiently influenced by his upbringing and able to choose the direction he takes. Because there is no human culture that is not collective and (these days) national, this upbringing always takes place within a particular and unique national culture and environment. Every society, speaking its own language and acknowledging a historical heritage and development unique to itself, has its own traditions and practices and an awareness of qualities and possessions that differentiate it from other societies.

Israel, for example, is home to two national communities and societies – Jewish-Israeli and Arab-Israeli. In both societies, humanity is struggling against the dehumanization of nationalism, racism and male chauvinism, which drive people to do to others what they would hate to have done to themselves – to use others as a means to their own ends and apply rules of ethics to their groups alone.

A humanist education, which would have none of the above, stimulates our humanity by teaching "nationality" rather than "nationalism," as well as equality between the sexes. The central purpose of any humanist education is to play a key role in this process of turning children into humane adults. The process is a fusion of socialization, recognition and encouragement of the potential for humanity, and the absorption of values. The values that acknowledge the rights of individuals but also stress their obligations – to all human beings, to communities closer to home and to themselves.

A humanist education is woven from two apparently contradictory strands that are, in fact, perfectly compatible: (a) socialization: adaptation to society, its culture, values, laws and dominant beliefs; and (b) individuation: the development of an autonomous, critical mind, equipped to appraise arguments, laws and customs, beliefs and education systems, cultures and traditions, and the heritage of literature. A critical, rational mind can perceive and reject dehumanizing and immoral aspects of values and commandments.

Education can either encourage students to appreciate the wealth and variety of their own and other national cultures or it can erect walls that shut out foreign cultures, the world's great classics and universal values. A humanist education, by introducing students to works representing both their own and foreign cultures, enriches and enhances the quality of life, stimulates intellectual-spiritual activity, expands the students' universe of associations and introduces intellectual and emotional challenges. Indispensable to our capacity critically to appraise our environment and achieve self-fulfillment are the comparisons we draw between our own society and other cultures, past and present. Given this breadth of vision, we cannot be held captive to anti-humanist traditions and thinking: the strength in humanist values, tried and tested by generations of rational criticism, makes this self-evident.

An education that ignores the riches of Judaism and other civilizations and confines itself to vocational training stifles and contracts the recipients' spiritual world, condemning them to remain ignorant of Jewish, Israeli and world culture. Nor may one profit from the commercial mass media, devoid of intellectual or poetic content, which similarly turns its back on culture and conveys a hollow, one-dimensional impression of the world.

Secular Jews have to guide their children towards their humanity and equip them with the principles and necessary tools of judgement for identifying and opposing racism, nationalism and other inhumanities. Secular Jewry knows what it wants, but it has no clear vision of how to get there. Replacing that confusion with clearly defined principles, objectives and methods is its major task.

MAN AS THE CREATOR OF GOD AND MORALITY

Values, morality and humanistic education aim at the wellbeing of humans and the higher quality of human life, and this proposition is tested and attested by rational enquiry and argument.

A "value" is a criterion we use to evaluate and rank. Secular Jews believe that the twin objects of all human-made values are the good of all people and the quality of human life, and that values are ranked by the measure of their contribution to the quality of life.

Human beings are makers and inventors. Men and women, in their kaleidoscope of national and ethnic cultures, fashion their religion and its symbols in works of art and theology; they establish articles of belief and then reject them; they develop the sciences with which to explore natural forces and discover ways of controlling them; they design codes of ethics and conduct. They consider some codes to be of divine authority, others as man-made.

Every human civilization has created gods peculiar to itself. Everywhere, men and women have invented religions, their narratives embodied in ceremonial calendars and codes of laws and commandments. Some of these religions have embodied rules of social behavior and ethical conduct; others have remained at the level of cult and ritual. Some gods have demanded, according to their priests' interpretation, terrifyingly antihumanist devotion, such as human sacrifice. The ancient Jews of Jerusalem, who killed their children on Moloch's altars during the first millennium BCE are a relevant example.

With the advent of secularization, men and women finally started to acknowledge that it was they who had made the gods in their own image and likeness, and that it was they who had devised the laws, customs and commandments of society. This allowed organized religion to be evaluated in the context of ethical precepts. In Judaism, and the Western world in general, the last two centuries of the second millennium have put the laws of state, synagogue and church on trial. The charge has been the offence against the three humanistic precepts articulated by Hillel the Elder (the greatest of the sages of the Second Temple period and *Nasi* – president – of the supreme court of law) and the philosopher Immanuel Kant:

- Hillel – Do not do unto others what you would hate done to you.
- Kant – Each man is an end in his own right and may never be seen as a means to another's end.
- Kant – No rule is ethical which is not of universal application.

The special task of secular, humanistic Judaism is to apply these three precepts in judging and ranking any value or rule of behavior – individual, public or political – and any rabbinical ruling or pontifical pronouncement. They are master-values.

Brought up on the values of humanism, we may simply assume that these master-values rank over any contrary value. Their supremacy, however, is rationally demonstrable. A quick glance at historical societies reveals that every society that violated the three precepts – dehumanized its population – lost its vital power and collapsed into social and economic decay. The social, economic, military and intellectual inferiority of Communist, Nazi and other autocratic and totalitarian regimes was obvious in comparison with free societies, or those in the process of freeing themselves from autocracy. Evaluation of historical evidence demonstrates that a slave society dehumanizes both the enslaved and the enslavers, brings about a decline in individual quality of life and arrests societal and intellectual progress.

THE FREEDOM TO INNOVATE: NEW LIFESTYLES, NEW FESTIVALS

Secular Jews express their beliefs in the ways they lead their lives and celebrate the festivals of their national culture. A Jewish lifestyle has always been recognizable by its celebration of the calendar's festivals and holy days and its observance of the *mitzvot* and special prayer services. Though each community or denomination had its own form of celebration, there was enough in common to make the festival manifestly Jewish. We believe, said the religious in their ritual and prayer, in a cultural-historical heritage based on the Bible, in our shared fate as a persecuted or barely tolerated minority living in exile, and in a common hope for a better future when we return to our own land. We believe that the inherited customs and *mitzvot* by which our community marks its festivals are holy.

To single out particular days for commemorating special events is a universal human need. Secular Jews satisfy this need by devising new forms and content for ancient festivals, in harmony with their current beliefs. Liberated from the obligatory prayers and practices grafted on by inherited custom, and considering themselves legitimate heirs to the Jewish historical-cultural legacy (without acknowledging that it has a sacred component), they are free to select the elements they wish. They choose the poetry and joy they still feel strongly connected to, discard what has lost its meaning and add new material and activities from other sources, as they deem relevant.

The Passover *Seder* is a good example of changing traditions. Secular Jews do not burn the *khametz* (forbidden leavened food) just before Passover but honor the festival as a celebration of the national liberation story and the new spring season. The readings they recite, the ceremonial and freely chosen content of the

Passover *Seder*, are compiled from the cornucopia of Jewish literature and song – contemporary, medieval and Biblical, traditional – in Hebrew or any of the other languages in which Jews have written. Anything that gives pleasure and joy can be incorporated, anything that enriches the spirit and expresses the festival's meaning in the here and now.

What were once holy days are being transformed by secular Jews into occasions for family and communal festivity. The festivals of the Jewish calendar have been evolving throughout history. For centuries, Passover was a sacrificial festival celebrated within the family, and for centuries after that it was the occasion for pilgrimage to the temple, where sacrifice was made for the whole people. Later still, for hundreds of years, it was moulded into the family *Seder* along the lines of the Greek *symposion* (a time set aside after a banquet for convivial drinking and discussion). Its format then followed the *Haggadah* compiled in the ninth and tenth centuries. The twentieth century has taken Passover into a new era.

Many secular Jews are unwilling to give up the Sabbath and festivals, despite the difficulty of finding appropriate new ways to celebrate them meaningfully. They acknowledge that an annual calendar replete with days for rejoicing, resting, and self-examination is far better than one in which every day is similar to another. Festivals give meaning to the cycle of time and the daily routine for communal celebration. Secular Jews have combined tradition with innovation to create festivals that still resonate with poetic and social meaning. Their celebrations give them cause to peruse ancient texts that might otherwise remain unread.

Twentieth-century Jews composed new *Haggadahs* for Passover, and ceremonial texts for *Tu B'Shvat* (the New Year for Trees) and Israeli Independence Day. Some of these efforts were printed in the tens of thousands; others were simply used by the immediate family. (In the Middle Ages and Renaissance, families would commonly embellish the *Haggadah* with illustrations and stories of their own, adding a private dimension of meaning.) The traditional *Haggadah* is a masterpiece of scenario writing that provides the family with a detailed framework and content for its *Seder*. Its composition was clearly influenced by the Greek *symposion* (the reclining position, the four cups of wine, the mix of song and verse, feasting and intellectual talk, the *afikoman* game). The two heads of the great *Yeshiva* at Sura in Babylonia (present-day Iraq), Rabbi Amram in the ninth century and Rabbi Saadiah in the tenth, gave us our best-known *Haggadah*, some two thousand years after the festival had emerged in its earliest form. The Amram–Saadiah "production," in several versions, was used for the next thousand years throughout the Jewish world.

It is more than a little remarkable that this "traditional" *Haggadah* (sections of which are in Aramaic, one of the languages spoken by Jews in the Rabbis' time) does not mention Moses. Moses, the key player in the event, which the festival was established to commemorate and celebrate – the Exodus from Egypt – was simply deleted. Yet the epic life story of Moses and the Exodus from slavery to freedom, and the role of both in the founding of the Jewish people, constitute the mainstay of Jewish humanism and its self-defence against its detractors, a point that Erich Fromm and Michael Walzer have amply demonstrated. In the twenty-first century, their two epics are still the core of the collective historical-literary memory that gives Passover its meaning. So it is hardly surprising that the dominant trend in modern *Haggadah*-making is to restore the figure and story of Moses to center stage.

Modern-day *Haggadahs* are amalgams of ancient and contemporary texts that combine the narration (plus commentary) of Moses's life story with poems, songs, legends, *afikoman* games, feasting and talk about the festival's contemporary significance. Some have restored Passover's link with the seasonal spring festivities in which it originated by including the text of the Song of Songs, a work of secular erotic poetry that tradition has attached to the festival.

Haggadahs like these give new life to the festival and highlight its historical-cultural origins. Also important are the works that it has inspired and that contribute to general world culture, such as the writings on Moses by Martin Buber and Sigmund Freud, his portrayal in stone by Michelangelo and Pisano, the libretto of Schoenberg's opera *Moses and Aaron*, the Hebrew poet Nathan Alterman's "Songs of the Ten Plagues" and *The Kid from the Haggadah*, and the poems and songs of Chaim Nachman Bialik, Naomi Shemer, Yehuda Amichai and others.

The "traditional" *Haggadah*, outdated and foreign to contemporary readers, was "traditional" for only one of the three millennia in which the festival has been celebrated. A new tradition is now taking over. The way secular people choose to celebrate the Passover is outstanding evidence of how celebration gives concrete form to what people believe. We see in the secular *Seder* their complete assurance that they are full co-heirs to the Jewish people's historical-cultural legacy. We see a stand on freedom of choice and a belief that tradition needs to adapt with time. The Midrashic texts that supplied core passages for the *Haggadah* of Amram and Saadiah are now being replaced by passages from the Bible, and Aramaic is giving way to Hebrew and English. Where earlier versions exalted Yahweh as the prime mover behind the Exodus, the new *Haggadahs* place the emphasis on celebrating freedom and a new spring for the current generation of Jews, who themselves played a role in their people's national liberation.

NEW WAYS TO CELEBRATE LIFE-CYCLE EVENTS

Most secular Jews (mainly those living in Israel), who would much rather celebrate a birth, bar- and bat-mitzvah, marriage and death with new rites, are, for lack of adequate alternatives, still being pressed into the rabbinical mould – circumcision, a synagogue bar-mitzvah ceremony, marriage by a rabbi, and burial by a Jewish religious burial society.

The vast majority of secular parents still circumcise their male children in the traditional rite, stifling their objections to a religious ceremony and surgical operation performed by a non-medically-qualified *mohel*. At death, the secular in Israel likewise tend to submit to an Orthodox funeral, unable in a time of grief to counteract the monopoly of religious establishment's officials at most recognized burial grounds.

The bar- and bat-mitzvah and wedding celebrations of secular Israelis, usually conducted by a rabbi, often have no meaning for the party concerned. A bar-mitzvah is often the first and last time the boy and his parents set foot in a synagogue. Israeli mothers are, by tradition, forced to sit in the women's section, separated from the ceremony, and the portion of the Torah chanted by the boy is determined by the calendar, regardless what he might find meaningful.

Wedding ceremonies held under Israeli law are conducted on behalf of the secular government by an Orthodox rabbi. (Israeli law does not sanction civil marriage.) The marriage contract itself, drawn up in the outdated form of a *ketubah*, is written in incomprehensible language following an ancient religious formula that is insulting to women.

Secular Jews are increasingly trying to find alternative and meaningful ways of marking rites of passage, where ceremonies are personally designed and conducted, free of the constraining presence of the civil servant-cum-priest of established Orthodoxy. Religious rites alone no longer mark the reception of a new child, male or female, into family and community. Resistance to circumcision itself and especially to its associated ritual has been growing over recent years, and attempts are being made to devise an alternative celebration for births of sons *and* daughters. Many newborn are being "inducted" into the bosom of their family in the conspicuous absence of a rabbi and fixed prayer service and without the ceremonial circumcision, itself a survival from an era of idol worship (the origin of which may be traced to ancient Egypt). Though various models been have been tried (communal singing and blessings on the family itself, rather than on God), no particular form of ceremony has yet achieved the status of a "new tradition." The Redemption of the First-Born (traditionally, the first-born son is consecrated to God or the service of God and has to be redeemed by the parents with a token offering of money) has, with good reason, disappeared from non-Orthodox Judaism. Other examples of attempts to secularize life-cycle events are the following:

Bar- and bat-mitzvah: Increasing numbers of secular families are arranging their own ceremonies. Though these take a variety of forms, a fairly constant element is a topic or issue within Judaism chosen by the boy or girl and prepared for presentation before the family and/or community. The ceremony is the culmination of a period of learning, so that the boy or girl understands what he or she is talking about and the Judaic significance of the event. The ceremony underscores the fact that this transition from childhood to adulthood is a universally celebrated human rite of passage.

Marriage: About a quarter of all Israeli couples now travel abroad to marry. The trend is gaining popularity among non-Orthodox Jews, who choose to be married by a Reform or Conservative rabbi, not currently recognized by the Jewish State. The Israeli parliament and government are coming under strong public pressure to break the Orthodox monopoly on official marriage, part of the process to separate the civilian and religious establishments.

Death: The same sort of pressure is slowly loosening the stranglehold of the Rabbinate and its contractors on burial of the dead. Secular burial is now fairly widely available (having recently been made legal by a Supreme Court decision), and there are now urban cemeteries in which the mourners, not the Rabbinate, choose how the funeral is to be conducted. Outside of Israel, Jews make their own choices regarding funeral arrangements.

A NEW JEWISH CULTURAL IDENTITY

Two hundred years ago, Judaism took on a culturally oriented direction – it began negotiating with the modern world and its new ideas of civic and social identities. The innovations described above are the natural culmination of this trend, sometimes more successful outside of Israel than within it, yet alive and relevant nonetheless. They represent Judaism's transition from a dominantly religious culture to an essentially secular one.

SECULAR JEWISH CULTURE

The changes now taking place in Jewish culture had their roots in the beginnings of the eighteenth-century *Haskalah* movement led by Moshe Mendelssohn. The movement adopted the ideas of Spinoza from the seventeenth century and began to relate to Judaism as the culture of the Jewish People and to *Halakha* as a body of laws that are subject to change.

In the second half of the nineteenth century, Judaism adopted the process of secularization. The *Haskalah* movement and other nationalist secular movements began to influence increasingly wider circles through new journalism and literature that broke the bonds of religious culture. A growing number of Jews released themselves from traditional community organizations and from their obligation to obey its leaders and the *mitzvot* of the *Halakha*.

Over the course of the twentieth century, the population of Jews who do not observe *mitzvot* became the majority of the Jewish population in Israel and throughout the world. Secular Jews were responsible for most Jewish creations in the twentieth century, and most Jewish youth (the majority located in Israel since the 1990s) attend secular schools.

Changes in Jewish culture and education in the nineteenth century left their stamp on thousands of Eastern and Western European Jews. With the waves of immigration from the East to the West at the beginning of the twentieth century, millions joined the ranks of the secular Jewish population in the large cities of Europe, America and the small *Yishuv* (Jewish settlement) in pre-State Israel. Centres for secular Jewish education and culture were established, producing thousands of non-religious works that renewed the visage and history of Judaism.

The process of secularization radically and comprehensively changed the lifestyle of Jews: their dress, food, sexual behavior, number of children and their style of education, spoken and written language, enrollment in institutions of higher learning, community life, use of time on the Sabbath and holidays, relationship to the *mitzvot* and Jewish sources, awareness of a national Jewish identity, openness to world cultures, professional options, exposure to the journalism and literature of many languages, and acquaintance with secular and religiously shunned works of art and research.

The lives of some non-Orthodox Jews who continued to observe *mitzvot* were also affected by these changes. In many cases, their lifestyles and thinking were similar, even identical, to those of the secular Jewish majority. A comparison between these groups and the ultra-Orthodox Jewish community that perpetuates the lifestyle prominent before the secularization of the nineteenth century illustrates the magnitude of this revolution. The reason was the nature of *Halakhic* Judaism, which, in its most orthodox form, dictates every detail of individual lifestyle and aims to seal individuals in a spiritual and educational ghetto.

THE ACCELERATION OF SECULARIZATION IN THE NINETEENTH CENTURY

In the last quarter of the nineteenth century, secularization gained speed among the majority Jewish population of Eastern Europe, then under Russian, Austrian and Prussian rule. Many Jews were introduced to approaches very different from what they had previously known. The ruling powers offered a general education for Jewish children at every level, including the university. Jewish enrollment quickly rose beyond the equivalent Jewish percentage of the population. Capitalism spread through Europe, and, caught in the friction between landowners and farmers, thousands of Jews were pushed from their feudal, village-based way of life into rapidly growing industrial cities.

Jewish men and women joined the proletariat of the developing class of hired workers in factories and workshops. As a result, the traditional community began to crumble, counterbalanced by an increase in the need and desire for education outside a religious Jewish framework. The *Haskalah* movement, which spread from Germany to Eastern Europe, supported new educational laws, despite the opposition by the ultra-Orthodox.

Jewish journalism and literature – in Hebrew, Yiddish and Russian – was virtually free of Orthodox Jewish influence. They produced articles and literary works that criticized traditional Jewish culture and education. Newspapers and journals spread information about international politics and economics, scientific and technological advances and intellectual achievements. Hebrew and Yiddish publications reached the hands of yeshiva students who became one of the leading forces behind the secularization of many young Jews who left the yeshiva and were exposed to the secular culture of Europe and America.

Hebrew and Yiddish journalism and literature produced "communication communities" of educated Jews, referred to by Israel Bartal in his research on changes in Eastern European Judaism in the nineteenth century. Jews who subscribed to identical newspapers or journals were exposed to the same information and experienced the same new ideas and sensations. They became drawn to each other intellectually and artistically. Over time, educated consumers of books and journals formed the basis of nationalist secular movements that developed among the people of Central and Eastern Europe. This was also the beginning of a wide range of secular Jewish culture – literature, theater, music, the plastic arts, historiography, philosophy and education.

THE "CLASSICISTS" OF SECULAR JEWISH LITERATURE

The first generation of secular Jewish writers were, for a few brief decades, the "classicists" of secular Jewish culture. They were backed by the nationalist movements and Hebrew and Yiddish education systems established in pre-State Israel and the Disapora.

The "free [of religious content] Jewish schools" that grew out of these movements offered an alternative curriculum to that of religious schools and non-Jewish schools. The works of the great new Jewish writers, who wrote in Hebrew and Yiddish at the end of the nineteenth and beginning of the twentieth centuries, laid the groundwork for the new Jewish secular culture. The works of writers such as I.L. Peretz, Mendele Mokher Sforim, Shalom Alecheim, H.N. Bialek, Saul Tchernichovsky, Ahad Ha'am, Y.H. Brenner, M.Y. Berdichevsky, and Martin Buber were considered by the new nationalist movements of the early twentieth century to be the harbingers of free Jewish culture. In this sense, these writers became the "classicists" of secular Judaism, owing to the literary value of their works, which endured and influenced many generations, and to the role they played in creating the institutions of the new Jewish culture.

The works of the "classicists" gave expression to the spiritual and social crisis resulting from the revolutionary change from traditional religious Judaism to secular Judaism. This literature (particularly works by Mendele Mokher Sforim and Shalom Alecheim) strongly criticized conservative Jewish society and its effect on the lives of individuals and families, as well as the naïve or ecstatic religiosity of Hassidic and other religious Jews. These are treated, as in the works of Peretz, Buber and Agnon, as part of a spiritual era that has passed. In the same generation, Bialek was considered the national poet. His poetry lyrically expresses the pain of the disintegrating internal world of the yeshiva, the helplessness of Jews threatened by pogroms, and the passive obedience to religious tradition. His works express a new approach to the myth of the Bible as an expression of the national tragedy and suffering of redemption, and they carry the message of freedom from belief in God's assistance.

Alongside the criticism, many new Jewish literary works describe the transition in Jewish life from religious to secular through satire, irony, humor, lyricism, romanticism, angry shouts and tragedy.

Though this culture draws from generations of Jewish sources and its many conflicting streams, its common denominator is the belief in Judaism as culture that continues to exist and develop in an era when secular Judaism replaces religious Judaism. The works of this culture all aim to offer secular Jews a spiritual and emotional experience that influences their lives as meaningfully as the religious experience.

NATIONALISM AND HUMANISM

The secular nationalist movements that also began to develop in the second half of the nineteenth century had, by the twentieth, become mass movements. The thinkers and leaders of these movements strove to meld secular nationalist ideals and humanism in the form of socialism or liberalism, based on the European humanistic model. The works of Moshe Hess, Herzl, Nordau, Zhitlovsky, Borochov, A.D. Gordon, Ben Gurion and others typified the struggle for justice and humanism of nationalist Jewish movements. Each suggested a solution for freeing the Jewish People from their status as a minority – either tolerated or persecuted – in countries controlled by either the left or the right. Waves of anti-semitism spread through Eastern and Western Europe in the nineteenth century through laws restricting the academic or professional development of Jews. There were blood libels – charges that Jews slaughter Christian boys for use in making *matzot* for Passover – as well as accusations of treason or international conspiracies (as in *The Protocols of Zion*, which was a popular work among Europeans early in the twentieth century and among Arab nations until today).

The meeting of these elements awakened and strengthened

Orthodox Judaism as well. It opposed emancipation, general and professional learning, nationalist and Zionist movements, openness to European culture, and the values of humanism as the ultimate test. This extremist conservative approach was shared by all Orthodox Jewish movements – the *Haredim*, the *Hassidim* (and its various communities of the "righteous"), the *Mitnagdim* (which opposed the *Hassidim*), the *Cabalists*, and the *Messianists*. The conservatism, introversion, and the idea of the "Chosen People" of Orthodoxy drew heavy criticism from secular Jews and prompted them to struggle for freedom of choice and universal humanistic values as the preferred alternative to religious and nationalistic values.

Secular Judaism, like Orthodox Judaism, was characterized by different ideological factions surrounding the following issues:

Humanism and nationalism: Some held that all policies and movements are to be judged according to their promotion of humanistic values and human rights, while others held that the nationalist interest is overriding.

Zionism: Zionists believed in the establishment of a national home for Jews who will either choose or be forced to live there, while anti-Zionists believed that Jews are people of the world who have existed most of their history outside the borders of Israel. The latter continue to claim that Diaspora Jewry must be strengthened as independent centers of Jewish life that are not dependent on Israel.

Jewish education: Secular Jews believe that Jewish education free from the bonds of religious tradition is based, like all Judaisms, on the Bible. This foundation of knowledge also includes a selection of sources from different streams of Judaism in every generation, including Talmud.

Belief in God: Secular Jews maintain that humanity is the creator of God and holds sole responsibility for maintaining morality and social justice in the world.

The Jewish community: Some Jews believe that religious communities must be replaced by secular ones in order to provide institutional, social support in the form of communities that celebrate Jewish festivals and life-cycle events at the individual level. Others, secular believers, see individualism as a component of secularism that is in conflict with the essence of any community. They see loosely organized groups of friends or families as the answer to the social needs of men and women.

These various secular points of view hold an essential belief in the development of the mind and spirit, which can be promoted through the free choice of individuals, as long as they fulfil their obligations to the societies in which they live.

CENTERS OF SECULAR CULTURE IN ISRAEL AND THE DIASPORA

The waves of mass immigration to the large cities of Eastern and Western Europe, and the immigration of millions of Jews to the Americas following pogroms at the beginning of the twentieth century, created new social and cultural centers of secular Judaism. In these centers, secular Jews established frameworks for primary, secondary and post-secondary education, professional associations and political parties that conducted social and political activities often based on conflicting views. Some groups published daily newspapers and established mutual-aid societies for European Jewish immigrants to the US and Britain. These centers of Jewish life produced many cultural works in Hebrew and Yiddish, the languages then spoken by most of the world's Jews. These were then seen as the languages of an autonomous Jewish culture developing in the Diaspora.

The smallest center of secular Judaism to develop at the start of the twentieth century was in pre-State Israel, whose Jewish population then numbered only a few tens of thousands. The secular Jewish *Yishuv* became a separate Hebrew-speaking society that included independent educational institutions. Though prior to World War One only 1 percent of the world's Jews lived in Israel, they believed the land would become the political and social fulcrum of the entire Jewish people.

Hebrew became the language in which secular Jewish residents of the *Yishuv* spoke, studied, and created. Only the ultra-Orthodox opposed the revival of Hebrew as a modern language, and they continued to speak Yiddish in their daily lives and in their study of the Torah, as some continue to do today, beginning at the kindergarten level. Secular Jewish culture developed before the establishment of the State of Israel in 1948, and it formed the basis for the cultural life of the country after the population grew to ten times its size, becoming almost 40 percent of world Jewry.

From the end of the nineteenth century to the Holocaust in the mid-twentieth century, secular Jewish culture flourished in the fields of literature, philosophy and theater. More than 18,000 Yiddish titles appeared in the 60 years preceding the Holocaust. Most of this writing was secular and humanistic in nature and in the critical messages it carried. It was aimed at Jews undergoing the crisis of transition from traditional communities, closed off from the rest of the world, to open societies in large cities. Among its authors were Sholem Asch, I.B. Singer, Itzik Manger and H. Leivick.

The twentieth century produced hundreds of books, poems and plays by secular Jewish authors – from Proust and Kafka to Saul Bellow and Primo Levi – writing in many languages. Those writing in the languages of Europe were integrated into the world cultures surrounding them, yet without losing their national identity (both in their own eyes and in the eyes of their host societies). Those who considered themselves fully assimilated and unconnected to the Jewish People were forced to acknowledge their roots as a result of the anti-Semitism that developed in the first part of the twentieth century and reached its peak in the persecution and killing of Jews sanctioned by European governments – in Germany, Italy, France, Romania, Hungary, and all other national entities that cooperated with the Nazis or forbade refugees from crossing the borders into their countries.

"JEWISH CREATORS" – THOSE WHOSE LIVES AND WORK ARE INFLUENCED BY THEIR JEWISHNESS

Secular Jewish culture is expressed in written, artistic and musical forms. The sum total of these works is greater in quantity and variety than those produced by Jews of all previous eras. The largest centers of Jewish culture in Europe were destroyed in the Holocaust, together with the Jewish societies that gave birth to them. Jewish cultural centers in the Islamic countries of Africa and Asia disappeared when their members emigrated to Israel and to the West. The centers of secular Jewish culture in the US – which produced daily Yiddish newspapers, schools, theater, professional associations – have either disappeared or shrunken considerably. This, despite the fact that the majority of the world's Jews are still located in these centers, free of the restrictions of a religious Jewish lifestyle and free to choose the way in which they want to educate their children and view the world.

Efforts began at the end of the twentieth century to revive Jewish communities in the West. Without massive enrollment in Jewish schools, the use of the Hebrew language and daily life in a Jewish cultural environment, Diaspora Jewry as a community has had difficulties in reactivating secular Jewish cultural centers.

CHAPTER 3

THE SPIRITUALITY OF SECULAR JEWS

One of the grave dangers facing secularism in general, and Jewish secularism in particular, is the apparent loss of spirituality or even the perception of its need, as if spirituality somehow needed to be "religious." However, secularism, in the full sense of the word, welcomes and even generates spirituality in manners that are worth noting. Disregarding the obvious human *need* for spirituality will only open the door to religion. The secular agenda must include a reaffirmation of spirituality in humanistic education and a sense of community and culture.

To people living in the world of the practical – "chrematistics," as Aristotle calls it (*chremata* being "objects" or "possessions") – everything seems exchangeable for something else. Exchangeability becomes the measure of a thing's value. People who desire success in the practical world evaluate everything by its price, that is, by its exchange value. Each single thing is perceived as belonging to a set or category of things, the category defined by the properties common to all its items. Since the invention of coins, price defined in monetary terms has become an abstract, impersonal and comprehensive concept. It allows for everything to be exchangeable for everything else. Massive quantities of print and cyberspace are devoted to the exchange rate for commodities, currencies, stocks and bonds, reflecting the population's increasing interest in such matters.

Living in a world of practicalities can conceal a world in which persons and things are not exchangeable but are an end in and of themselves. Their place in our lives cannot be exchanged. To be aware of this dimension requires a developed capacity for experience – taking pleasure, for example, in literature, art and philosophy – or for friendship and love. This other dimension reveals itself in artistic, scientific and spiritual creativity, personal relationships of family and community, our national culture and the legacy handed down to us through the generations.

Our ability to reason is dependent, of course, on concepts, generalizations and categories that sort items into classes. Knowledge and understanding depend on the ability to attach a class name to a mass of particulars ("animals," "human beings"), to derive rules of behavior by which acts and ideas can be judged ethical or unethical, and to affix a single price to things that differ in every other respect. While the power of rational thought, understanding and evaluation is vital for life in the practical world, it is equally vital to that power of moral, critical judgement that enables us to evaluate and rank, and then endorse or disqualify, all behaviors, laws, beliefs and attitudes.

Our power to feel is contingent on our ability to discern the particular and unique within the mass and to develop our capacity for experience through encounters with the particular. It is the virtue of the particular to carry us beyond that which can be generalized to mental-spiritual contact with reality and nature, with others living among us or in works of art. Thus, our need for spirituality is just one expression of our longing to break the bounds of the practical world and re-enter the real world, the world of unique experiences.

"Spirituality" is one of the names we give to those times and experiences when, in a world crowded with exchangeable *objects*, our spirit makes contact with a reality composed only of *subjects*.

There are "particular" works, artistic or literary, that are unique and broader than any genre or collective definition can encompass. The response occasioned by a work of art or literature is inimitable, not exchangeable, and it retains its potency in our spiritual life. A Talmudic saying captures the distinction between a world of fabricated images and the uniqueness of divinity:

> All kings forge their image and likeness on the coins they mint and all these coined images are alike. The King of Kings, on the other hand, imprints his image and likeness on every human being in the world – and each one of them is unique and unrepeatable.

Most people never experience great works of art. Complex and unique works of art and science are expressions of the "higher culture," which most people do not see in their community institutions or learn about in grade school or college.

The greatest works in the Bible, classic Greek and Shakespearean tragedies, the novels of Tolstoy and Dostoyevsky, the paintings of Rembrandt and Leonardo, the sculpture of Michelangelo and Donatello, the music of Bach and Mozart, are particulars that express and illuminate a universal reality and inspire an experience of a kind beyond rational explanation. When creations and experiences like these are absent from the spiritual world of most people, who live as "mass consumers" rather than "citizens of a community of culture," it follows that the craving for spirituality will grow more intense.

As faith in religion and political ideologies crumbles, the desire strengthens for a spiritual dimension to life. People living in relative material security become attentive to the non-material insecurities of their psyche. With the collapse of faith in the traditional religions and in a personal God whose commandments have been directing their lives, some former believers discovered a void at the heart of their spiritual world and found themselves, as Erich Fromm puts it, gripped by the anxieties that freedom carries with it. With the collapse of faith in utopian political ideologies and their ability to redress the world's injustices, some political believers also found themselves in a vacuum of uncertainty, with their lives lacking any sense of purpose.

In both these communities of ex-believers, the angst and sense of loss are keen and there is a growing desire for a spirituality (as yet undefined) that can heal them.

Some of these utopian political ideologies were humanistic, preaching the absolute goals of justice, equality and liberty for all. However, the way some socialist regimes chose to realize them trampled both the values and any promise of a society that promoted the welfare of all its citizens. Murderous dictatorships not only disillusioned people to ideology itself, but also undermined their faith in the possibility of translating humanist ideals into reality. A new ideology of material cynicism seems to be spreading fast, replacing "values" with calculations of practical utility. An ideology that preaches a society and economy built around unregulated competition and the privatization of services renders its leaders deafer than ever to the needs of the poor and weak. Surrendering totally to the calculations of efficiency and profitability that rule the practical world, politicians and other leaders lose sight of a world where people yearn for values.

One response of the Western educated elite to this societal trend was a renewed search for spirituality, for unmediated communication with the particular and the singular in human beings, with acts and words whose value lies within and is not exchangeable. This search sometimes manifests itself as volunteerism in organizations working to protect the physical and social environment and in the huge interest shown in mysticism, alternative philosophies and esoteric practices.

Many people in the West today are looking for activities and lifestyles that can generate spiritual experience and take them beyond the mundane. Large numbers of secular people have sought spirituality in the civilizations and religions of the Far East. Others seek *Kabbalah* studies or turn to the new communities of Jewish faith (New Age, Jewish Renewal) which, through rituals, community singing, close interpersonal contact and strong communal bonding, aspire to restore an emotional component to the faith or to emulate Hassidic fervor.

While such seekers of spirituality, religious and secular, do not see eye to eye in their definition of what they seek, they are nonetheless of one mind that the level of spirituality possible in their current lives in Western civilization is inadequate. The routine of their lives lacks stimulation and challenge, something to lift them to a higher spiritual level. In *mitzva* observance, they no longer find a sufficient answer for their ethical and spiritual needs. Neither in modern education nor rational thought can they find intellectual justification for the current tenor of their lives.

Rational behavior engages only part of our mental and spiritual capabilities. Intellectual development geared only to rational knowledge and judgement exhausts our capacity for experience and does nothing to spark emotional and spiritual response. It is a response to what lies beyond the rationally explicable – sublime creations of art and literature, the awesome beauty of a vast natural landscape, the encounter with a rare and captivating personality.

Men and women cannot have a spiritual life without engaging and developing these mental and spiritual capacities. These capacities enhance life; they bring a person face to face with the *misterium tremendum*, with the sublime that exists in both the human and natural worlds. When the capacities lie dormant, dissatisfaction and boredom ensue.

Three main developments have made secular people, Jews and non-Jews alike, feel such a need for a spiritual dimension to their lives: the break-up of communities, a cultural diet composed entirely of mass entertainment, and schools that have replaced cultural education with vocational training.

When communities decline into mere television audiences, their members are left feeling alienated. No social institution has stepped in to replace the role of the synagogue as a community center. What are commonly known today as "community centers" are, for the most part, quite unequipped to function as active centers of a neighborhood's communal and cultural life. Most Jewish community centers shut down on the Sabbath and holidays, which severely restricts their role as a focus of community life. This loss of a regular meeting place, owned by and operated for the local community, available at all times, is one of the factors in the disintegration of local community life.

Until the end of the nineteenth century, active membership in a community was an essential part of human life. In modern Western society, this communal fabric was ripped apart. Community membership is a spiritual matter, bonding an individual not only to a group of people, all of whom know and acknowledge each other as group members, but also to a historical community, stretching back for generations.

This second communal allegiance is the nation or tribe, ethnic entity, people or one of the other terms applied to an amalgam of smaller communities united by a common cultural heritage, language, territory and so on. These "communities of culture" also acknowledge as members the deceased of previous generations. The head of a small Jewish community in the Atlas Mountains of Morocco once explained to the Israeli documentary-film director Arnon Tzafrir that his community "numbered twenty-five thousand persons, of whom three hundred were still living." Tombstones, pictures and photos, names, stories, songs and ceremonies of remembrance keep the dead present in the community's spiritual environment. Many ancient religions were built on ancestor worship, raising their former patriarchs and matriarchs to the status of divinities.

A "community of culture" ensures that its education nurtures communal continuity and solidarity and awareness of the community's history, traditions and key figures in its heritage. The community's story becomes central to its cultural heritage, and it is shaped and colored by written texts and works of art, festival rituals and traditional customs.

The spiritual-intellectual crisis of secularization has given rise to questions about the purpose and meaning of life. Today it is apparent that the search for a purpose to life and the desire to break the "bounds of ego" are signs of a crisis of meaning. From these fundamental questions flowed numerous others, questioning the justification for pain, suffering and human life itself. It was to seek justification for human life that Albert Camus set out to develop his own philosophy. The very existence of the debate betrays the dissatisfaction of people whose material needs are met, but whose lives remain empty.

In essence, however, there is no answer to questions regarding the meaning and purpose of life. Human life is its own purpose, not a means to an end, but an end in itself. Liberation from the sense of meaninglessness in life comes with the knowledge that one plays a significant role in the lives of others. This is a paradox that demonstrates the futility of egoism – knowing that our actions have a positive effect, that they occasion happiness and pleasure, helps generate a sense of purpose. So sure are some individuals that their actions are vital to the community, nation or humanity, that they are ready to sacrifice their own life for a purpose.

That is indeed one of the paradoxes of life: that the individual is exalted and filled with a sense of meaning when what he or she does is of meaning to others. Efforts on behalf of family, community, nation or humanity itself are just an extension of the same idea, equally or even more capable of generating a sense of purpose and a readiness to give of oneself. Put differently, the paradox is that men and women need to break the bounds of the ego in order to bring the ego to fulfilment. What is love for one's partner in life if not one of the greatest expressions of this fundamental element in human nature?

The ego's very awareness of itself is, as Martin Buber states, the product of the bond that develops between the "I" and the "thou" in the other. A baby begins to recognize itself as a result of the bond it builds up with the human "you" in its mother or father. The desire to go beyond this, to break away from the ego, is one of the loci of our spirituality, one of the drives that make us do more than is necessary for our physical and material needs.

There are religious persons who identify the "other" with the god characterized by earlier generations of their culture and community. This is an "other" that, they believe, has to be appeased. Many religious believers say that their sense of meaning comes from their devotion to this divine "other" and the sacrifices they offer for his sake.

Biblical prophets, however, warned against forms of worship, sacrifice and prayer that ignored our duty to the *human* "other." Cultic observance that neglects our duties to social justice becomes, in their view, meaningless and hateful to God. The prophets Amos and Isaiah capsulized this view with the words, "... even though you offer me your burnt offerings and grain offering, I will not accept them ... but let justice roll down like water, and righteousness like an everflowing stream" (Amos 5: 22, 24) and "... even though you make many prayers, I will not listen; your hands are full of blood. Wash yourselves, make yourselves clean, remove the evil of your doings from before my eyes, cease to do evil, learn to do good, seek justice, rescue the oppressed, defend the orphan, plead for the widow" (Isaiah 1: 15-17).[1]

The covenant between God and Israel rests on the duty of every man and woman to the human "other," and this duty has precedence over cultic obligations. This explicit precept in ancient Judaism, as expressed by prophets such as Amos and Isaiah, deemed justice and charity more important than sacrifice and prayer to Yahweh, who, in their view, does not want them.

The secular position is that gods are the creation of man; they are symbols of human potentialities, of the desire to be all-powerful, to escape the limitations of the ego, to be of meaning to the other, and to give life itself a meaning and function. Unfortunately, the gods of the many religions created by humans have symbolized and represented both sides of human potential, malevolent egotism and the urge to aid others in their adversity. One of the ways in which this latter tendency expresses itself is in a sense of responsibility for the other. Our response to this sense, says Martin Buber, is evident in both our outward expression and our inner core: "Once a baby has put his hand in yours, the responsibility for him is yours."

A SECULAR PERSPECTIVE ON THE RELIGIOUS RESPONSE TO THE NEED FOR SPIRITUALITY

Yosef Dan sees the Lurian (Rabbi Yitzhak Luria) system of *Kabbalah* as a successful attempt to spiritualize the observance of *Halakhot* at a time when Jews were questioning the grounds for continuing to do so. A new conceptualization of God was winning adherents: he was no longer a personal God to be prayed to and whose "will" had to be done, but an abstract being with no capacity for speech and certainly no need for petitions and sacrifice. This left Jews with the problem of explaining the "grounds for the *mitzvot*," a problem to which neither Saadiah nor Maimonides had given a satisfactory answer.

Building on the Zohar, Lurian theology endowed *mitzva* observance with universal meaning and purpose by assigning it an essential role in returning the wheel of creation to its starting point. The Jewish people would restore the world, shattered at Creation when primordial light had rushed into the void left by the withdrawal of God, causing the sparks of good to fall and embed themselves in the shells of evil. The Jewish people had a duty to bring about the world's restitution by strict observance of Torah and *Halakha*. They were charged with raising up the sparks again, rescuing them from the shells of satanic evil, redeeming the Godhead from its self-exile, thus restoring the universe to the point preceding Creation – the absolute harmony of Nothingness.

In one stroke, this system proposed wiping out the revolution brought about by Biblical Judaism by replacing the universally held concept of time (as an endless cyclical succession of the seasons) with the linear concept of time as history, the world evolving towards a future state. Egyptian and Mesopotamian civilization, imprisoned in the cyclical concept, reduced man's role on earth to helping to keep the cycle of time turning, since all that would be had already been, and all that had been would return. Biblical Judaism had countered this notion with a point of universal genesis, from which the history of man and his world moved away, changing incessantly, never to return to any past point or state. The cyclical concept was conservative, while the Judaic concept looked forward to change and unprecedented development. It sowed the seeds of opposition to the conservative worldview, set in motion the drive for the constant regeneration of tradition and provided the vision that inspired the innovators of the Oral Law, the great reforming minds of Hellenistic Judaism, the rationalist movement of the Middle Ages, and the *Haskalah* of the modern period.

Lurian *Kabbalah* proposed a counterrevolution. The Jews were to be removed from the advance of their own history, and of other peoples', and bound again to the role of maintaining a divinely ordained cosmic cycle. Unforeseeable renewal and regeneration were replaced by a return to cosmic prehistory, to the restored pre-Creation harmony, in which there is nothing that is not God and nothing changes. Lurian *Kabbalah* is indeed an ideal vehicle for those who want to escape from the real world into fantasy. In contrast, secular life finds its spirituality not in escapism, but in involvement in social and cultural life, in the profound experiences this life furnishes us and in a receptivity to change.

That the books of the Bible make no mention of a next world or a life after death is sufficient evidence that Biblical Judaism was entirely focused on the problems of this world. While Judaism's early neighbor religions placed faith in life after death in an alternative world at the core of their system, to the Yahwist prophets it was clear that justice had to be done in the here and now, there being no other time or place for people to enjoy its benefits. On this same basis, modern secular ethics requires men and women to work for the good of the other and their society in the here and now, and the fulfillment of these obligations of justice and support is one of the sources from which our lives and acts draw meaning.

Many caught in the crisis of meaning look in vain for relief, to escape from the reality of this world into communication with the next. When mysticism and its teachers promise contact with, or some form of entry into, a world beyond this one, they are offering an out-of-body spirituality, a way for us to experience the next world without quitting this one. An increasing number of Westerners spend time in Indian ashrams or at Buddhist retreats, or immerse themselves in the teachings of Jewish *Kabbalah* or turn to healers for spiritual sustenance. Many emerge disillusioned from such experiences, feeling their spiritual world may have found some peace but little new content that is relevant to their lives. The outcome of a mysticism that turns people's minds away from the world in which they live sometimes results in further alienation from their own society. A state of temporary bliss is perhaps to be had from these types of spirituality, moments of mystical oblivion from the world and its content. Any ecstatic activity produces this effect by anaesthetizing the rational side of the brain. But the effect passes and the dilemmas remain.

Similarly, by carefully observing the religious commandments and restricting study to works sanctified by tradition as the source of the mystical in Judaism, people are cut off from their own society and culture. Shutting oneself off from contemporary civilization only impoverishes the capacity for a wider spiritual experience and exacerbates the sense of meaninglessness.

THE SECULAR RESPONSE: A NEW EMPHASIS ON THE COMMUNITY

It is meaningless to ask about the "purpose of life" since the question has no answer. Since life is its own purpose (as are pleasure, nature and love), our life has meaning not when we know "the purpose of life" but the purpose of our acts. That is how the author of Genesis 1 understood the purpose of life when he composed his account of how life was created. Life was created to live: it was not ascribed a function to fulfil, an end to attain. That idea was the invention of Genesis 2. In this second version of the Creation, God brings every living thing into the world with a function and purpose. Brought to life by the breath of God, the first creature, man, is created to be the tiller of God's garden; all other creatures, woman included, come later to relieve man's solitude.

Searching for purpose in what is, by nature, purposeless is futile and can do nothing to mitigate the feeling that life has no meaning. Yet, though life itself is functionless and meaningless, within the framework of our lives there is room for many roles and functions that give meaning to what we do and how we live. Acknowledging this meaning is one strand of our spirituality, one that is uplifting when we judge that we are leading a good and useful life, and depressing when we feel we are doing no good.

This constant evaluation of the usefulness of our actions is a distinct but essential part of a life of experience. Our belief that self-evaluation must be imbued with a strong element of reason stimulates us to endow our ritual activity with new customs, to enrich it with the resonance of our own experience and time. Secular Jews have, in this way, been revitalizing Jewish festivals and celebrations for the last hundred years.

This form of mental-spiritual experience is in no way like the meditation intended to empty the mind of conscious involvement in current reality, one that identifies consciousness with a nothingness and void purported to bring relaxation and tranquillity. The mental-spiritual life that fuses sensation, experience and reason is of particular importance to us for two of its properties: it gives us pleasure and excitement by using memory to infuse pleasurable events from the past with present meaning and uses our capacity for imagination to conjure into mental reality people and things we have never seen.

However, none of this leads automatically to happiness. Happiness is not a realm of contentment in which we can dwell by spiritual means alone. Happiness does not visit our lives only in fleeting (though sometimes recurring) moments of contentment; it is also the outcome of knowing that the way we are living our lives is bringing real benefit to others. This sort of life is possible only when we pour the whole of our selves, mind and body, into it. Mere devotion to the self, a life of exercise in "pure spirituality," designed to empty our consciousness, does not lead to real happiness.

One of the ways in which the longing for the spiritual manifests itself is in our urge to escape the "boundaries of the ego." Early forms of social organization set a rigid structure for the extended family and the tribe, society's institutions. They unilaterally determined what each individual's place and role had to be.

After exile, migration and urbanization broke up the tribal form of organization many of these early social institutions collapsed and were replaced by new forms of social involvement, not contingent on clan or tribal membership. Jewry invented and developed a new pattern of social organization we can call a centralized "community of culture," that is, a community acknowledging a single and unifying cultural heritage revolving around a place of assembly, which we know by the Greek name "synagogue." Early synagogues were the focus of a range of sociocultural activities, as well as of religious worship, and it was only much later in history that religious activity became the synagogue's key function. This new social invention, spread far and wide across the globe by Christianity and Islam, was the predominant and pre-eminent setting for Jewish life for the two thousand years of the Jews' dispersal. It began to break down only in the nineteenth century, overwhelmed by mass emigration, secularization and the rise of nationality-based aspirations.

"Community," in the sense of this synagogue-based unit, is at once abstract and tangible. On the physical plane, it is composed of individuals known to each other and meeting frequently. On the mental-spiritual level the activities performed in its context are interwoven with the core concepts of tradition, nation, faith and an ancient inherited culture. The degree to which community membership impinges on the individual depends on the degree of his or her involvement in and awareness of communal institutions and cultural life.

The longing for a spiritual dimension to life, which takes the form of a desire for social contact and belonging, is often satisfied by joining a community – religious or secular – and participating in activities that lift the individual beyond the ego. An active social life within a collective enables us to realize our particular self through the special contribution we make to the collective, and which the collective acknowledges. Without a communal framework to acknowledge our individuality, most people find it hard to be of meaning to others and to win acknowledgment of this meaning.

The kibbutz movement in Israel was the first and the most extensive attempt in history to create entirely secular communities that embrace all outward facets of individual life. Now, early in the twenty-first century, 250 of these communities are still active in Israel, despite all the radical changes in character and internal organization that they have undergone. This is still the largest secular Jewish community that brings up its children in the Jewish heritage without religion and poses its individual members with the far-from-easy challenge of communal life.

The enjoyment and excitement that move the participants in a social gathering are transparent expressions of the mutual nourishment of the social and spiritual. The need to bond with others and relinquish the ego, if only for a while, locks exactly into the need to feel the reality of the spiritual dimension. The tokens of this bond must sometimes appear trivial to the observer – community singing in which individual voices merge into the general chorus, the physical contact of holding hands in song or other group activity. These gestures, however, are part of the way people express the sociability they need so deeply (at a time when even dancing has become something done alone in the presence of others).

A great variety of communal organizations partially fulfil this traditional function of the original community. People bond for a variety of purposes (social, artistic or political), feeling through their devotion to the group enterprise the satisfaction they seek in emerging from the boundaries of the self.

KNOWLEDGE AND BELIEF

The relation of knowledge to belief epitomizes how religious and mystical sects aspire to achieve spirituality in ways different from secular humanists. For secular Jews, belief and knowledge are mutually reinforcing; for the religious and the mystics, they are contradictory.

Secular humanists can rise to the spiritual plane because they recognize and welcome the ability of men and women to devise new realities, both physical and mental-spiritual. An example of a man-made mental-spiritual reality of enormous power and influence is "God" and all the other literary heroes and heroines who have achieved reality in our mental world. This confident conviction in humankind's spiritual and creative potential, in the moral heights men and women can reach – mirrored in the evil to which they can sink, for they have a sovereign power of choice – is an empirical conviction, based on knowledge of what humankind has already created and done. Our belief that the natural laws human scientists have discovered possess universal validity is reinforced by our knowledge that humanity has the ability to know more and more about the physics of the universe and that the internal logic and external predictions of these physical laws have stood up to centuries of objective testing.

Similarly, our belief in the validity of certain moral values, as expressed in the precepts of Hillel and Kant discussed earlier, and the principles of democracy and human rights implied in them, is reinforced by knowing what has happened in democratic (as opposed to dictatorial) regimes – by historical evidence for the superiority of the quality of life under regimes ruled by these moral values.

"Belief" is a conviction about what ought to be, about the binding validity of certain human-made moral principles and the values engendered from them. "Knowledge" is recognition of what is, a tangible or mental-spiritual reality; it is recognition of the result of testing laws and commandments by measuring them according to moral criteria and practical implementation.

Experiential knowledge is exposure to the unique, to that which cannot be generalized or quantified. Part of experiential knowledge is asking oneself the meaning of the natural or man-made phenomena experienced. This questioning and wonderment goes to the very core of our mental-spiritual activity. It is one of the ways we give our lives a spiritual dimension.

Secular humanist belief and faith generates enormous inner power and fervor, driven by the desire and hope of doing some good, allowing people their freedom, giving each individual equal opportunity to realize the potentialities of his or her humanity – in education, social activity and social activism, and the creative work that inspires genuine mental-emotional excitement. This sort of belief demands knowledge, from which it draws strength and tests itself. It uses knowledge of what is, in order to bring about what ought to be. Knowledge and rational judgement are essential to it. Of course, the secular have an inestimable advantage, since what ought to be has not been set in stone for them by divine sanction: they have the privilege of changing their minds about it.

Faith without knowledge, belief that declines to be tested

against or anchored in knowledge, leads the believer to lose touch with reality. Political ideologues have refused to acknowledge the possible and have deliberately ignored the limits and structure of human behavior and mentality. Some, for instance, have tried to set up supranational states, disregarding what history teaches them about popular aspirations for national independence. Their faith in universal brotherhood has blinded them to evidence that nationality, ethnicity and tribalism are still what they always have been, decisive forces that determine the fate of political arrangements or governing regimes.

Faith without knowledge can also be hazardous to sanity, if we define sanity as the ability to differentiate between reality and unreality, between the possible and the impossible. In the worlds of those mystical sects whose faith turns on scorn for the laws of nature, believers are urged to believe their appointed messiah is alive after he is long dead and buried, or that they can command spiritual power to overcome bodily limitations. Bit by bit, the boundaries between faith and knowledge crumble and the realities of this world are left behind. Self-immersion in these mystical sects, and in the blind faith that they offer the only path to the good life, releases participants not only from the problems of earthly society but also from its culture. The masterworks and spiritual world of its great scholars and artists seem to be irrelevant to them. Thus, while secular beliefs draw nourishment and conviction from their roots in human reality, the spirituality of mystical religions removes itself from knowledge and from any enquiry into the realities of life.

Knowledge and faith add meaning to one's career and personal life. A sense of vocation motivates us to work for others; the confidence that we are fulfilling our vocation uplifts the spirit. *Haskalah* Jews felt this exaltation when in the seventeenth and eighteenth centuries they strove to free other Jews from the authority of organized religion. Socialist and nationalist revolutionaries felt they were struggling to free a people or class from repression. Religious missionaries are buoyed by this sense, believing that in converting a child to their own religion they are saving a soul.

Knowledge without belief and faith, however, is no less dangerous. "To know that" (information) and "to know how to" (skills) is not "to know why," that is, to know what one's information and skills are to be used *for*. This requires a kind of belief. "To know that" and "to know how to" is to have a certain conception of reality and how to cope technically with the challenges it sets. "To know why" requires belief because, having recognized what is, we must then choose what ought to be. As faith needs knowledge to test the realism of its aspirations, so do knowledge and knowledge-getting need beliefs – to help choose a field of study, set goals and evaluate the relative importance of bits of knowledge to human welfare.

Faith based on knowledge encompasses faith in the importance of doubt and criticism of every assumption and premise. Only by doubting and criticizing can we approach a more truthful concept of reality, or change it according to new discoveries.

SECULAR BELIEF AND THE INSEPARABILITY OF THE SPIRITUAL AND PHYSICAL

The spiritual and the physical/material realities in man are distinguishable yet inseparable. To spiritual reality we ascribe abstract concepts, ideals, consciousness, experiences and feelings. These are things we are aware of mentally; they are an essential part of being human, of human nature and structure. They remain an essential part of our reality even when they are labelled "transcendental," that is, located somehow over and beyond our physical reality. Yet the spiritual is not to be separated from the physical in man even if it exists on a plane beyond the tangible and the immanent and even if we perceive it within an experience that words cannot adequately describe. Spiritual experience, such as love for a human being or wonderment at the universe or for a piece of music or a painting, is something we have no doubt is real since we feel it as an inseparable part of us, though it is not part of our corporeality.

"Spirit," "mind," "soul," "mentality" are labels we give to the plane where our spiritual realities exist. Yet these realities are an inseparable part of our whole personality and we do not sense that they possess a separate existence. Even physical pain or pleasure, physical in the moment of its happening, becomes, in the expectation or memory of it, a spiritual reality.

The God-fearing authors of the Bible are of one mind with atheist thinkers today in refusing to accord the soul or spirit an existence separate from the body. All the content and events in our minds are not a *"Deus in machina,"* as the English philosopher Gilbert Ryle explained in his book *The Ghost in the Machine*. The "spirit," "mind" or "soul" is the totality of all the mental-spiritual activity of our personality fused with the body's physical movements and workings.

LOVE, FAITH, AND ART – THE THREE PILLARS OF SPIRITUALITY

The desire for spirituality – in the sense of a dimension to life extending beyond the rational, a life dense with profound experiences – manifests itself in love, art and faith. All three are mental-spiritual concepts with the power to lift a person out of routine and beyond the boundaries of the ego, beyond an exclusive concern with satisfying bodily needs and appetites.

Love for an individual or community, for a people or all humanity, evokes a feeling of rising to some higher level and spurs us to do things unconnected to any material advantage (even leading us, at times, to act to our material disadvantage). The feeling of being part of a family or community is one of the most basic expressions of solidarity with the other and the human need for a bond that "comes with no strings attached." Love is one of the forms in which Buber's "I" bonds to the "thou": the "I," discovering the uniqueness of the other, enters not into a *relationship* contingent on circumstances, needs and interest, but into a bond of affinity uniting us directly with a living personality whose unique qualities stimulate and enrich our spiritual life.

Love as an exciting and exalting attachment can take many forms: the love of babies for their parents, of parents for their children, of adults for their life partners. It can also take the form of love for a close friend, alive or living after death in our memory. It can be love for a work of art or for the characters (human or divine) created by authors and artists. The longing for spirituality is in one sense a longing for love. People suffering from a loveless life or who have lost touch with family and community, people who have no access to artistic experience, all yearn for love.

As the Enlightenment and secularization left their stamp on European culture, including its extensions outside Europe, a crisis developed in the traditional faith in God and his commandments, punishments and rewards. The revolution of the Enlightenment and secularization undermined prevalent educational dogma but raised few alternative forms of education to embody belief in human sovereignty and in man as creator of all gods and values. Many, now disillusioned with divine faith, felt that their world had lost all spirituality.

The education systems of secular societies have not faced up to this change in the structures of belief and faith. Most secular teachers and students have little or no idea of the beliefs that their way of life expresses or of the works of literature and art that are part of their secular culture. One result of this lack of awareness of the new basis to faith and belief is that the longing for spirituality often goes unnoticed.

THE I–THOU BOND, REACHING FOR THE SUBLIME AND REALIZING THE VALUES OF HUMANISM

"It is not good for man to be alone," says the author of Genesis. To break the limits of solitude, men and women need "the other." Martin Buber differentiated between our relations to the other as "it" and our affinity to "thou." For the most part, our relationship with "it" is functional, for the sake of some*thing* but not some*one*. There is a practical endpoint: obtaining a service or a good. The "it" in these relationships is exchangeable, like any service provider or trader of goods, and there is nothing in such relations to break the individual's solitude.

I–thou relationships, by contrast, are our paramount source of spirituality. Each relationship is unique. Each partner to it discovers the "thou" in the other, his or her unique personhood. Moreover, as the relationship unfolds, each one discovers his or her own "I," just as every child discovers his or her "I," as a result of the developing bond to parents. This is the relationship that takes people out of the solitude into which every human being is born.

According to Buber, we can form a bond not only to a human other, not only to an animal we are attached to by love, but even to a tree, a mountain or a god, whom Buber conceived as the "thou" in the universe itself.

Love, artistic creativity, the emotional power of a work of art, a living faith in the humanist ideal of rescuing people from misery – all these are "I–thou" relationships capable of elevating us to a higher plane of mental life. They animate and enrich our spirit, awakening our deepest feelings and carrying us beyond the limits of ego and into identification with the beloved.

Group solidarity is another such "carrier." People form groups and communities to achieve some ideal, united by a common faith and program of action, such as a national liberation movement and social revolution. Groups such as these release individuals from solitude and give them the confidence that they are helping to bring about historic events; they impart a sense of meaning to their lives.

It is this conviction that men and women are capable of the sublime – a capacity quite inseparable from their equal and opposite potential for egotism, degradation and evil – that motivates humanists to realize their ideals. Humanists believe that the innate superiority of human beings over other forms of life lies precisely in this freedom of choice between two paths and also in the ability to create new choices. Men and women can pursue either the ideals of humanism or the gratification of their self-seeking instincts, which may be racist or nationalist, chauvinist or murderous. Their potential for the sublime is in this power to conquer base instincts and genetic dispositions, overcome limitations and disabilities, achieve great social and artistic creations, create gods, moral values and other symbols of their aspiration – to create a new human environment distinct from the natural one.

Men and women express their capacity for the sublime through their belief in ideals and their efforts to realize them. Over three thousand years in the making, these ideals belong as much to the realm of the emotions and compassion (a form of profound mental-spiritual bond and commitment to every human individual) as to reason and rational judgement. In the spiritual life of secular believers, the bond to the other and the pursuit of ideals are two sides of the same coin.

COPING WITH THE CRISIS OF MEANING

Victor Frankel singles out yearning for a more spiritual life as a frequent reaction to the "crisis of meaning." It is one of the gravest crises humankind has had to deal with since the author of Ecclesiastes declared, "Futility! Futility! All is utter futility."

Meaning, says Wittgenstein, is what we call the function ascribed to words that seem to us meaningful, such as the words that guide us accurately to some address or destination. Meaningless words are those that may seem to offer guidance but cannot fulfil their function, that is, cannot guide us correctly to our destination.

The extent to which we feel our lives have meaning is bound up with our evaluation of the functions we fulfil in family and community, in our work or in any sphere where we feel our acts and their product deserve acknowledgment. We usually get the greatest sense of "meaning" when what we do influences others and reverberates in their lives, when we anticipate gratitude or at least believe it is deserved. Social and religious activities, scholarship and artistic creativity, also occur, for the most part, in a societal setting and are directed towards others, with the expectation or hope that they will respond to or acknowledge the contact, even if the response is not immediate. The meaningfulness of our acts is connected, therefore, with our rational dimension: we perform them in the belief that they serve a useful purpose. Reason weighs their possible consequences and calculates the potential benefits to others.

From the same rational source, Jews question the reasons for adhering to the *mitzvot*. Whom does *mitzva* observance benefit and how? Is it God? Is it ourselves? We may adhere to the *mitzvot* for many reasons, out of faith, habit or respect for a time-honored tradition. Maimonides, in his discussion of the *mitzvot* of animal sacrifice, explained that Jews had persisted in this particular practice because, having become habituated to it in the days when they worshipped "other gods," they, like all human beings, could not pass quickly "from extreme to extreme" but had to be weaned away from the custom gradually as they came to understand that it brought no benefit to God or man.

As secularization penetrated Jewry, the seeds of doubt sown by

Saadiah and Maimonides took root and spread. Secular Jews, having outgrown their belief in the necessity of appeasing God in favor of a conviction that the correct goal of life is pleasure and welfare, abandoned the *mitzvot*, for which they could find no reasonable justification. From this point on, rational enquiry was directed to deciding what duties all men and women were obliged to respect and fulfil and what *mitzvot* they should maintain for the good of humankind and themselves.

The desire to win the recognition and respect of others is but one expression of the deeper need to feel our acts have meaning. To feel this "meaning," then, to sense that our lives have a point for others and not only for ourselves, we have to break out of our inner solitude and take up our roles in society. The tension deep in human nature between egoism and altruism is reflected in our need and wish to satisfy our selfish desires by giving pleasure, satisfaction and benefit to others. To take pleasure in their respect or gratitude, we have to believe that they value what we have done.

THE SUBLIME IN HUMANITY AND HUMAN CREATIVITY

At the root of any spiritual experience, declares the Hellenistic philosopher Longinus (*On the Sublime*), the primary cause of the exhilaration of the spirit we feel at the splendors of nature and of human art is the encounter with the sublime.

Nature shows us the sublime in the awesome, vast desolation of the desert, where the prophet Elijah met God as the "sound of thin silence." In human art, the sublime is evident in the masterworks of individual men and women who, representing the whole of humankind, occasionally bring us a unique work that is complex and dense with meaning, a work that is the voice of both a singular personality and of all humanity. Masterworks like these – in all fields of art, science and scholarship – reverberate through history in their revelation of the heights human beings are capable of reaching.

It is only in these splendors of the creative imagination that humanity's potential can achieve any sort of definition, even if that very creativity sometimes exposes the murderousness and degradation that is also human. Faced with such sublime creations, we stand amazed at the power of exceptional people to perceive reality in a unique light and vision – to use symbols, ideas and images to create a new reality and expose new aspects of the physical world and the human condition.

It is in the world of culture that we encounter the great creations of the human mind. In the modern era, works of art of all ages and civilizations congregated to form the contemporary culture we live in. Members of one culture can create in the spirit and method of another or fuse artistic and scientific elements from a number of cultures. For those granted the opportunity to enjoy such a creation, it becomes a great revitalizing secular spiritual experience.

Some cultures encouraged and even obliged their members to know their civilization's greatest achievements. Some of the masterpieces of Judaism are read on the Sabbath, festivals and holidays, so that the experience of them is relived: Genesis at the New Year, Jonah on the Day of Atonement, Ecclesiastes on Sukkot, the Song of Songs on Passover, Ruth on Shavuot.

It is the great good fortune of Israeli Jews that they speak the classical language in which some of the masterpieces of world culture were written. Schoolchildren can read the books of the Bible as they were written over two thousand years ago. The opportunity to experience the sublime spirituality of a secular love poem such as the Song of Songs, the poetic rhetoric of Isaiah, the masterly narratives of Genesis, and the religious poetry of the Psalms, should not be wasted by presenting these works to students exclusively as collections of signs and symbols for linguistic or archaeological analysis.

In the new reality created by a literary or artistic masterpiece, hero and heroine struggle with the cruelty, injustice, pain and affliction of human life, drawing strength from whatever mental and spiritual powers they can discover in themselves. That reality is the expression of the capacity to wrestle spiritually with life and create a stable reality within the endless flow of moments and events that come into being and die in an instant. It is when these masterpieces become part of our spiritual experience, part of what is hidden from us in human nature, that we touch the sublime.

THE CO-EXISTENCE OF DEGRADATION AND THE SUBLIME

Humanists are no less inspired by their beliefs and spiritual commitment than religious believers by their devotion to God. However, humanist vocation and compassion coalesce not in God, but in sublime art and poetry, because these allow communion with all humanity.

All religions have made use of works of art to express and stimulate faith and encourage the bonding of the human "I" to the divine "thou." Many classic literary texts that convey religious experiences inspire works of art, such as the Sacrifice of Isaac, the Book of Job, the Book of Ecclesiastes and the tragedies of Prometheus and Medea. These were created in an era in human cultural evolution when religion and religiosity were dominant.

Divine religion and secular humanism sometimes draw nourishment from the same text, work of art, ritual or tradition, because of their power to raise us above the solitary human condition. Though Spinoza's religiosity declared itself in his love for the divine and the sublime in nature, he did not accord his religiosity an existence separate from nature.

Our capacity to bond to a mental entity, such as God and other literary heroes and heroines, or a deceased person still alive in our memory, is common to the mental and spiritual life of both the religious and the secular. From the Hellenistic period on, atheists concluded that this is how God came to be a presence in the human mentality. Men and women refused to reconcile themselves to the death and disappearance of mothers, fathers or great leaders, and they kept them alive mentally, eventually attributing to them a reality outside the reality of memory. When one of these figures appeared in a dream and seemed so real as to exist outside the workings of the mind, then, even awake, dreamers could well convince themselves that the figure was a presence in the real world and not only in their minds. If an author or artist then recreated the actuality of that figure, now a vivid presence in their admirers' waking hours, the heroes and heroines of memory sprang to new and autonomous life.

Belief in the autonomous divine existence of such figures – alive in the memories, dreams, myths, literature and art of their believers – melted away; what remained were the magnificent works of art created by the believers. The worshipful relationship to "Our Father in Heaven," to a mother-goddess or to "the King of Kings" is an element of this process. In retrospect, God-fearing philosophers such as Aristotle, Maimonides and Spinoza, who perceived God to be an abstract concept, synonymous with the "Unmoved Mover," can be counted among those who hold that a personal God is no more than a creation of human spiritual creativity, a figment to which ancient authors ascribed reality, will, personality, and the capacity to create and to destroy, to command and punish.

God and other literary heroes continue to live as mental-spiritual constructs in readers' minds, and the texts that gave them being remain what they always were – vehicles for a vision of human potential at its most exalted and its most depraved.

THE FUSION OF RELIGIOSITY AND ATHEISM IN SECULAR JUDAISM BY EINSTEIN AND BUBER

Albert Einstein, a believer in Spinoza's God, in "the divinity of the natural world," wrote that Judaism embodies "an intoxicated delight in the beauty, wonder and sublimity of the universe, of which man can perceive only a pale shadow." For Einstein, this delight and wonderment were the source of the spiritual power animating all true research and "could also be found in bird-song." For him this source of power is what represented the most exalted aspect of the idea of God.

Martin Buber, whose thought represented a milestone on the road towards a fully developed secular Judaism, believed that man has the capacity to form a relationship not only with the human other but also with natural phenomena. Just as Longinus saw the sublime as much in a natural panorama as in the products of the human spirit, so Buber believed that men and women could discover the "thou" in their natural environment and transcend the limitations of the rational ego by discovering their affinity with nature. Here lay the core and essence of Buber's religiosity.

Believers in Spinoza's God do not see themselves, as Sigmund Freud, Sidney Hook, Y.H. Brenner and Haim Cohen do, as atheists in the sense of deniers of the idea of God. Their "secularism" is of the kind that demands freedom from organized religion and its laws. The two groups unite in their belief in the sovereignty of man and the absence of any duty towards divinely attributed commandments. Both see the superiority of man to animals in the capacity and need for a spiritual life. In this unique capacity to rise above his animal nature, they perceive one of the challenges that evoke the spiritual in man.

THE ROLE OF IDEALS AND SECULAR MESSIANISM

The best and happiest life for the greatest number of people is an ancient humanist ideal reflected in many religious visions of redemption and a Garden of Eden. For humanists, it is the highest moral value, the yardstick by which all other values and all behaviors, laws, commandments and regimes are judged and ranked.

The "good life" is also an essential element in all humanist utopias. In Judaism, messianism derives from the tradition of biblical prophecy, which articulated Yahweh's covenant with Israel as a society that must be ruled by social justice for all. In the modern period, numerous social movements (from the French to the Russian Revolutions) began by pursuing this humanist ideal but became corrupted by forcefully imposing the desired new politico-economic order. All possible means were justified, while the rights of the individual, guarantees of individual liberty and equality, and freedom of thought, expression and democracy went by the board. The results were often dictatorship and totalitarianism.

These particular failures cannot, however, detract from the ideals at the basis of all humanist idealism: a good life for all, guaranteed rights for every individual and ethnic group, and a world peace in which education and the development of individual spiritual and intellectual abilities assure the highest possible quality of life. Whether the utopia is envisioned by a national liberation movement or a social-change and social-justice movement, all these ideals play an important role.

Humanist ideals are ends in themselves, requiring no justification. The pursuit of happiness is one of the fundamental demands of the first declaration of the right to form the basis of a legal constitution, namely, the American Declaration of Independence, which conforms entirely to the ethical bases of Western democracy. These state that not only must we not do to others what we should hate done to us, but that we should show regard for all others and work in their interests, knowing that each is an end in him- or herself and never a *means* to an end. This applies, moreover, to every human being, without exception, for no precept can be moral that does not apply universally.

If the "good life" is the purpose and ultimate goal of morality, then appeasing God cannot be that goal, and man is free of any obligation to the religious commandments codified to enable us to "do God's will." In any dispute between secular and religious faith, pursuit of the good life here on earth is the deciding criterion. This connects secular humanism to the preference of the biblical prophets for social justice over religious ritual.

The hostility of certain religious authorities to birth control – parenthood planned according to the resources of family and society – is the most obvious and destructive example of the harm that can be done by putting religious dogma before values that protect and nurture humanity. The battle for birth control and a woman's right over her body is only one facet of the struggle to attain equal rights for men and women in every sphere of life.

In contradistinction to Christian messianism, which aspired to redeem individual men and women from the curse of original sin and the punishment decreed for innate depravity, Jewish messianism has always sought redemption for the Jewish national collectivity in a world of peace. Secular messianism (such as socialist Zionism in the nineteenth and twentieth centuries) sought self-definition for the Jewish people and liberation from exile, both geographical and spiritual.

Secular Zionism is one of the few messianic movements in history that have realized the major part of their utopian vision. As Herzl forecast in *Der Judenstaat* and *Altneuland*, Zionism succeeded in founding a Jewish state that offered Jews who wanted liberation from their status as a tolerated or persecuted minority a secular democracy that accorded organized religion a place but not dominion.

WHAT DOES SPIRITUALITY CONTRIBUTE TO A GOOD LIFE?

Both religious messianism and various movements for the redemption of humanity from earthly suffering have set their sights on the good life that begins when this one ends. Other movements aimed to realize the vision in this world and this life.

In every era, humanists have argued over how to define the physical and spiritual "good life." Most modern secular humanists would point to physical, spiritual and intellectual activity, autonomy of personality, and freedom from the afflictions of loneliness and deprivation and from other sources of suffering and pain. Both Socrates (in Plato's early writings) and Aristotle (in the *Nicomachean Ethics*) knew that the pursuit of maximum pleasure can be destructive. Addiction to immediate gratification can also bring suffering, both to others and to the pleasure seeker himself in the form of damage to physical and mental health and a loss of freedom.

What is needed is a measure of reason in the choice between alternative sources of pleasure. The Socratean way is for wisdom to guide the mix of sensual gratification and rational consideration, so that desire becomes something willed and the quality of life is enhanced, even if part of that life must be unavoidable suffering. Socrates differentiated between acts of physical and mental gratification that cause harm even as they delight, and acts whose benefits are measured over the long term, even if the immediate prospect is pain.

Pursuit of the good life is an element of our active spirituality that cannot be satisfied by rationally selected acts. Our powers of reason and rational calculation are certainly a major factor in evaluating, ranking and making moral choices among what is offered for our good and pleasure; they are still only one factor, however.

Pursuit of the good life, then, is certainly not to be identified with hedonism, which is the pursuit of immediate gratification and the belief that no other goal is as worthy. Nor is it compatible with a life devoted solely to study and reason. The good life must contain experiences of the sublime beyond the power of reason to explain or words to describe.

A SPIRITUAL LIFE: HOLDING AND PURSUING IDEALS

We add a spiritual dimension to our lives and a spiritual direction to our efforts in education, public life and individual creativity by holding and pursuing ideals that protect and nurture humanity. The practical work required to turn ideals into reality makes us part of the human community.

The aim of ideals that impart meaning and have a spiritual dimension is to save our physical environment and ensure equal rights for all people. These ideals can be realized only if their pursuers strive *beyond* equalizing economic and legal rights by encouraging individual creativity and autonomy of mind and personality for the enrichment of the spirit.

THE ROLE OF EDUCATION

Entertainment has now taken over most of the leisure hours of Western societies. The types of entertainment are similar in form and in their aim to please. Works of art, broadly defined, such as the masterpieces of literature and art, are always unique. On one level they also generate pleasure; but they are infused with an excitement engendered by the encounter with the artist's unique stance towards human reality and ability to make the "impossible probable," as exemplified by *Oedipus Rex*, *King Lear* and *Faust*. Their plots could be the stuff of cheap melodramas. Yet in the hands of Sophocles, Shakespeare and Goethe they became what Aristotle considered poetic Truth.

An exclusive diet of mass entertainment leaves us spiritually starved. The thrills and spills, for all their ingenuity, fail to create the emotional-cerebral experiences that enrich the spirit and generate new bonds with Buber's other. Even the best entertainment delights by its ingenuity of form or plot. But this reaction stimulates only a tiny fraction of our spirit. The greater part remains hungry for stimulus and activity.

THE LOST GROUND OF EDUCATION

Most Western education systems and institutions train students for a career in a technologically oriented civilization, while largely ignoring the challenges of cultural education.

The term "civilization" encompasses the totality of those occupations and activities – organizational, medical, technological and financial – directed to meeting defined ends and evaluated by the results they achieve, their efficiency and the exchange price they can demand. "Culture," on the other hand, is all that we do in the realms of community and spirit. It is our scholarship, literature and art, social activity, rite and ritual, tradition and custom. While cultural activities are ends in themselves, they are not without purpose. They generate the experience and excitement of family and social life, an affinity to a cultural community past and present, and the encounter with natural phenomena and the great works of man. They give us quality of life, enrich our spiritual world, sharpen our senses and sensitivities and instil ethical and aesthetic values.

Human beings inhabit a plurality of "worlds," especially those of international civilization and national culture. Many education systems today train students for "tasks;" they concentrate on providing skills, such as computer programming, communication and language. Most schools do not provide the type of schooling that brings students face to face with works of high culture, the traditions and the beliefs of different peoples, moral dilemmas, individual rights and obligations centered on our primary moral values. Practical schooling and vocational training equip young people for success in the practical world. They do not give them sufficient points of entry into the culture and spirit of their own culture and others. Most importantly, students are not educated to be aware of their potential as human beings.

In the ancient world, even the uneducated masses were exposed, in theaters and temples, to the classics of their culture. Greek democracy obliged all citizens, excepting women and slaves, to take part in the social and political affairs of the community. A law attributed to Solon threatened punishment for citizens who did not take sides in political disputes. Greek tragedies (usually identified with "high culture"), were performed for mass audiences in their communities. Members of traditional Jewish communities had weekly encounters with Biblical literature. However, once these "communities of culture" collapsed and the experiences with "high culture" passed from the world, the gap between the few who retained access to high culture and the many who from time to time were treated to "entertainment" began to widen.

[1]*The New Oxford Annotated Bible* (Oxford: Oxford University Press, 1989).

CHAPTER 4

GOD AND OTHER LITERARY CHARACTERS

"Thank God, I am still an atheist."
Luis Bunuel

God was born in men's minds and has no existence beyond man-made literature and art.

The evidence for the gods' having been created by man is their being found only in man-made things – in books and paintings and theologies. The human mind knows only man-made gods. The "God" we know is a character in literature, a figure fashioned by story-makers and then represented to a believing public by every other art form humans have devised, painting, sculpture and mask, dance, pantomime and theater. There is not a religion in the world that has not had recourse to literature and the arts to represent its god and there is not a god in the world that has not been described in words and depicted in figure and form. Man's arts fashion the god's image and render its life and deeds in exciting narrative. They endow it with features and traits of character, with commandments and statutes.

In Judaism's literary classics, some human heroes and heroines actually meet Yahweh-Elohim face to face. Adam and Eve, Abraham and Jacob and Moses, so the Bible tells us, encountered him here in this world, the one world there is, so the biblical authors believed, the world in which we all live and die. Later compositions, the mystical *Merkava* and *Hekhalot* writings (dating to the first centuries of the Common Era) recount journeys made by R. Akiva and R. Ishmael to a second world. This one comprises no fewer than seven heavens and is the abode of Yahweh-Elohim, where he sits enthroned as a king over his court (a court, says the scholar of mysticism Joseph Dan, bearing a marked resemblance to descriptions of the imperial Persian court). In these tales of early science fiction Yahweh-Elohim is depicted encircled by hosts of archangels and ministering angels who govern the peoples and states ruled over by the King of Kings.

The myths and legends that manufacture gods by compiling biographies of their deeds and putting words into their mouths were a prime source for our classic masterpieces. The *Gilgamesh Epic*, the Garden of Eden narratives, the novel of patriarchs and matriarchs we call the book of Genesis, Homer's *Iliad* and *Odyssey*, all obviously draw on this source. We read these masterworks and our imagination fuses with the author's art to give life and breath to their word-fashioned figures. They enter our consciousness, possessing the same "existence" as people we remember or fantasize into being in day and night dreams.

The prophets and others who believe in "God" and in the words ascribed to him, because they have had a sleeping or waking vision of him and "saw" him in a form like the one they knew from books and other art forms, have had an encounter experience essentially no different from any other literature-reader's encounter with a well-drawn hero or heroine, be the hero/heroine's name Isaac, Penelope or Elohim. Both the religious and the non-religious (by non-religious I mean people liberated from obedience to religious commandments and from commitment to the reality of a personal god) meet Yahweh-Elohim only through the agency of human art and artistry. The one is no different from the other in knowing him as a living figure, who acts on human history only by dint of the belief rendered him by the selfsame people who devised and made him.

TO BELIEVE THAT GOD IS A LITERARY CREATION OR TO BELIEVE IN GOD, CREATOR, LAWMAKER AND RULER OF THE UNIVERSE

Freethinkers, also known as "seculars," are well aware that among Elohim's creators, the authors of the Bible's source materials, for instance, were many who were certain of his reality outside the texts they composed. He was Creator, Legislator, source of the *mitzvot*, king-ruler of the whole universe, and all-seeing controller of human lives. The laws and *mitzvot* they held themselves bound by they attributed to him, even though these laws were the formulation of human men, in Elohim's name of course. They were God-fearing men, these believers – that is, they feared Elohim's capacity for wreaking punishment, and hoped anxiously that he would reward their obedience to the *mitzvot* and *Halakhot* they ascribed to him and look kindly on their compliance with the rulings of every rabbi who, they chose to believe, spoke in his words or had the secret, more than other sages, of deciphering his will.

A belief system of this sort molds lifestyle and children's education, predetermines sex life, diet, dress and politics. The last, of course, will be the sort that fights to raise *Halakha* to priority over democracy and to nullify laws of the state daring to outface those of the *Halakhic* code. Believing instead that Yahweh-Elohim is a literary creation, conjured into existence only by the artistry of his human creators, one knows that the point of ascribing man-formulated *mitzvot* and *Halakhot* to "God" is to make the people feel bound by them ("a legal fiction," a former Israeli Supreme Court justice, Haim Cohen, terms it). With this knowledge comes freedom, freedom to choose to obey religious commandments or not and to disqualify or amend pointless and immoral *mitzvot* – which is precisely what secular Jews and the great majority of "traditional" and Reform Jews do. They ignore the greater part of the *Halakchic* code, select out the *mitzvot* that seem positive, and repudiate the immoral (those, for example, that discriminate against women or order the genocide of whole peoples).

The difference between believing *that* Yahweh-Elohim is a figure from literature and believing *in* Yahweh-Elohim as personal God and lawmaker is a gulf of principle between two conceptions of life, morality, democracy, education, Judaism and Jewishness. Believing in the creative powers of literature allows the values of humanism to assume supremacy (the values of Hillel, for instance – do not do to others what you would hate done to you; and Kant – only universal rules are ethical). From this position, it is clear that every law and *mitzva* must stand and pass the test of a universal humanist moral code and any that cannot – religious or otherwise – is at once null and void, no matter how many "words of God" stand behind it.

FICTIONAL CHARACTERS TAKE ON LIFE IN READERS' IMAGINATIVE MINDS

Breathing life into a word-fashioned figment of the author's art is one of the wonders that great literature performs for us (with our help). Before our very eyes the figments become personalities, distinctive and inimitable: they violate norms and morality, they are led astray by weaknesses, they struggle – some of them – against their fate; in other words, they are just like the reader, at least in potential. Yahweh, Abraham, Jacob, Joseph, Rachel, Yehuda, Tamar, Ruth, Jephtha, Saul, David, Jeremiah, the list goes on and on. Ajax and Hercules, Plato's Socrates, Don Quixote, Madame Bovary, the Karamazov brothers, Tolstoy's Natasha – over each one the magic life-giving wand has waved. But beyond the printed page and the reader's mind's eye their existence ends, unless another artist in another art form takes up the work of hero-molding, as Michelangelo did for Elohim and Adam, Picasso for Don Quixote, Shakespeare for Kyd's Hamlet.

Over the course of the first millennium BCE, authors and editors in Hebrew created Yahweh-Elohim, an exclusive and unique god of multiple images and personalities – creator and destroyer, inconsistent and by no means almighty, a sinner punishing sins, a regretter of deeds done, rescuing his chosen people, then deciding to annihilate them. Yahweh-Elohim is the collective hero of the "Collected Works" we know as the Bible, an anthology that opens with his creation of the world and humankind and immediately follows it with his original sin against the humankind he has created. This is the very stuff literary heroes are made of. Believable and familiar in all his foibles and failures, Elohim is the very embodiment of human desires and of human beings' megalomaniac aspirations to make and mend worlds.

ELOHIM'S ORIGINAL SIN – A KEY COMPONENT IN A VIVID LITERARY CREATION

Most of the world's great classics confront the reader with richly idiosyncratic heroes and heroines, who enthral us with the very audacity of their sinning – for which Plato proposed garlanding the authors with laurels and glory and then throwing them out of the city. Shame, for instance, is a trait that the solitary-living Elohim lacks totally. Men and women, in contradistinction, cannot do without it, something the author(s) of Genesis knew full well, for this is the first emotion the first two human beings feel after eating from the Tree of the Knowledge of Good and Evil. Elohim's great sin, committed with that characteristic total shamelessness, is to forbid Adam and Eve this knowledge of morality in order to stop them assuming God-like qualities.

Richard III, Dr. Faustus, Medea and other famous literary sinners captivate us in spite of ourselves. The list of sinning biblical heroes is also long. Abraham unhesitatingly prepares to sacrifice his son on the altar, Jacob cheats his blind father to steal his elder brother's birthright, Joseph taunts his brothers and father and mother with the dream of the sun and the stars foretelling his destiny to rule over them, Yahweh plots with Satan to rain destruction on Job and his family for no other reason than that Job, a pure-living and righteous man, deserves to have his faith tested by ordeal. Heroes and stories like these, revealing our capacity for sinfulness, have risen to symbolic status. A whole generation of Israeli parents saw in the Sacrifice of Isaac a metaphor for their readiness to send their children and grandchildren into battle and death, in defense of the Zionist vision they believed vital to Jewry's survival and redemption.

The Garden of Eden narrative (was it authored by a woman, as Harold Bloom speculates?) can be read not as Eve's "original sin" but as her rebellion against Elohim's original sin in trying to keep human beings from knowing good from evil. (How does Elohim respond but by imposing a curse on all women for all time, a curse encapsulating the sociobiological tragedy of women in a patriarchal society – enslavement to their menfolk, a life filled with the pains of childbirth, which only serve to increase their dependency and enslavement, and love and lust for the men who enslave them.) Jewish tradition followed Catholic (Augustinian) tradition in transferring the "original sin" from Elohim to Eve but the biblical text says nothing of the kind. On the contrary, it marks this successful mutiny as the major turning point in the history of humanity. Humankind learns morality and with it shame, the foundation of conscience. The mutiny liberates it from a prehistoric never-changing jungle and challenges men and women to begin creating a *human* civilization and culture.

As the Bible sees it, therefore, the onset of civilization is the onset of ongoing conflict between its divine hero, Yahweh-Elohim, and its human heroes and heroines. From Eve to Job the reader is witness to a succession of conflicts between humans and their "God," between humankind and the symbol of its aspiration to achieve the image of its ideal self – a mighty god wavering, like men and women, between lapses into sin and the making of masterful moral laws and ringing calls for social justice.

CHAPTER 5

HUMANISTIC VALUES VERSUS RELATIVISM

THE INCOMPATIBILITY OF PLURALISM AND RELATIVISM

In general, relativism argues for a non-absolute morality. It finds moral justification in every position and belief, on the grounds that behaviors should be judged by the moral code of the society that produced it. Many have pointed to the danger of this moral stance, noting that a relativist can morally justify racism, nationalism, male chauvinism, psychopathy and egotism – even when they threaten society's very existence. Thus, humanist pluralism cannot be relativist. It must take the position that men and women have the right to hold divergent, even contradictory beliefs and opinions, as long as their mutual rights are protected. Everyone must meet their obligations to society while allowing others to exercise their legitimate rights. Humanist pluralism can therefore never permit, as does relativism, one individual or minority to take power and subject a whole society to an antihumanist worldview.

As we have seen, the culture of debate has been a salient feature of Judaism for centuries. Moreover, the precepts of Hillel and Kant, quoted earlier, support a pluralist understanding of society – the legitimacy of coexisting beliefs and opinions and the right of every person to express his or her own beliefs. It goes without saying that these precepts do not condone the oppression, enslavement, humiliation, exploitation or silencing of others. Above all, religious dictates that draw their authority from beyond-human entities are unacceptable because they stifle debate.

Humanist pluralism allows societies to defend themselves against anti-humanism by making the interchange of ideas contingent on the obligation of each party to defend its opponent's right vigorously to broadcast and defend its own views. The corollary to legitimizing debate and controversy is delegitimizing every form of totalitarianism, which has a natural tendency to silence or destroy dissenters.

By definition, relativist pluralism that attributes equal justice to all sides yet permits authoritarian or monopolistic claims disqualifies itself. Also invalid is relativism that regards all description of reality as equally true, since it denies that a reality exists and is discoverable by research, debate and empirical testing. There can be no coexistence between humanist pluralism and relativist multiculturalism.

THE DANGER IN RELATIVISM: DEHUMANIZATION

In an address on human dignity in 1486, Pico della Mirandola said that man is the only living being with the gift of dignity, and that dignity originates in his capacity for choice. Every other being is born of a seed that fixes its character and behavior. Only man can be "like a beast in his instincts, like an angel in his wisdom, like a green plant in his indifference, and like God in his understanding of the universe, self-sufficient nature, and purity of conduct."

The relativist position that, within the moral framework and culture of the society that engendered it, every law or commandment may be accepted or recognized as "just" is a threat to individual humanity. A major trait that differentiates human from animals is their potential for both humanity and inhumanity. Dehumanization can manifest itself in psychopathy, mass hysteria, racism and the slaughter of one's own kind. The great problem with relativist tolerance for antihumanist values is that tolerance can be developed for phenomena such as Nazism, the killing fields of Pol Pot's Cambodia and the callousness of the Taliban.

Racism and chauvinism have allowed the members of one gender, race or nation to systematically deprive and abase the members of others. There was no justification for the tolerance shown to white Americans who forced blacks to sit at the back of public buses, and there is no justification for Israeli secular citizens to tolerate similar behavior on the part of ultra-Orthodox in towns like B'Nei Brak. The fact that a community approves apartheid of one kind or another is no justification for the resulting abasement of fellow citizens of a democratic state.

An essential ingredient of our humanity is the certainty that treating the other as we would hate to be treated ourselves, or regarding the other as a means and not an end, is morally wrong and cannot be made right. The mere fact that such habits have existed as "customs" for hundreds of generations is no justification for their existence. The relativism that lives comfortably with deprivation and humiliation on the basis of sex and race encourages individual and collective egotism, invalidates the presumption that all individuals in a society enjoy equal rights and, by logical extension, invalidates the demand on them to fulfil their obligations to society. This relativism threatens society's very existence as a humane and evolving entity.

A culture is formed by the accumulation of memories, traditions and customs, together with the more tangible products of human creativity and ingenuity. However, we cannot engage with the cultural life of our society, Jewish or universal (as Aristotle explains in his *Nicomachean Ethics*), without responding to the forces that animate our culture and without being socially and intellectually active ourselves.

To achieve a better quality of life, both children and adults should be educated in their national cultures and open to the world culture of which they are a part. By exposing us to the excitement and poetry in works of art and science, education leads us to seek stimuli for our minds. If our education (in and outside the classroom) also instils humanist values and a habit of social activism, then it enriches us all. The spiritual-intellectual activity generated by analysis and discussion of the heights and depths of human civilization leads inevitably to an awareness of the rights and obligations of individuals in society.

Each individual needs to be aware of trends and changes in national and world culture. The best way to achieve this end is to restore the ancient Jewish institution of "continual study" (*limud matmid*). The vehicles for this system of informal adult education were the daily study (alone or in a group) of a page from the Jewish sources, long-term study groups (*batei midrash*), and even whole months of study set aside by the community (*yarhei kalla*). It is a tradition well worth reviving, provided that its content expands to cover every subject area and medium of Jewish and world culture.

Continual study is an end in itself. It has no predetermined objective, such as academic qualification. Its aim is spiritual-intellectual exploration for the pleasure, stimulus and enrichment of the activity itself. It is one of the essential ingredients for the quality of life of children and adults, but not if it is merely yoked to the achievement of targets and titles. Constant learning should mean constant exploration of phenomena in the natural world and peculiarities of human nature and civilization.

The Ten Commandments, the Prophets' teachings on social justice and Hillel's master-value, show that Jewish humanism is an embodiment of universal moral values. Israel's Declaration of Independence and Foundational (Constitutional) Laws have sustained this tradition. However, in the practical life of Israeli society, breaches of these laws compete with their observance. A declining but politically powerful minority still defends and propagates antihumanism, in the form of discrimination against women and the expulsion of populations. Only by maintaining the ascendancy of its democratic and humanist strengths over its opponents has Israel achieved a higher rate of development than most of the new states formed after World War Two.

History demonstrates that totalitarian regimes destroy the fabric of their societies. Societies ruled by racist ideologies ruin their own economic, military and cultural-educational resources. The twentieth century's dictatorial and racist regimes all disintegrated through internal atrophy. History is on the side of humanism and pluralism.

CHAPTER 6

JUDAISM AS CULTURE: PLURALIST AND EVER-EVOLVING

JUDAISM AS A CULTURE

"Judaism" is a comprehensive term for the culture and civilization of the Jewish people. As such, it extends to all sectors of Jewry, both religious and free. Those who consider Judaism a culture feel separated by a chasm from those who consider Judaism a religion. Judaism, taken to mean the pluralist, ever-evolving culture of the Jewish people, embraces the whole of Jewry – the Jewish religion in all its manifestations and Jewish secular culture in its kaleidoscopic variations. Judaism as a culture is all that Jewish civilization has produced since Jewish history began, including the 2,600 years (beginning long before the "Exile") when Jews lived scattered among the nations of the world, absorbing and borrowing from all of them. Judaism is a culture of a "nomadic" people who, except for a period of a few hundred years, wandered from land to land, continent to continent and culture to culture. Unlike other nomadic peoples, however, who isolated their culture from outside influences (the Gypsies and Bedouin for instance), Judaism evolved in part by selectively adopting and adapting to the culture of its many hosts – the Egyptians, Babylonians, Persians, Canaanites, Arab Muslims, European Christians and the Western secular world. Despite this, the Jews never stopped developing their own national tradition, founded on a belief in their unique history and on their hopes for national redemption and restoration of their own land.

Until the eighteenth century, the predominant element in Jewish culture was religion, as it was in the Jews' host societies. In the nineteenth and twentieth centuries, with the majority of the world's Jews living in Europe and the Americas, the secularization that swept through the West and displaced organized religion affected the Jews as well. The realization of the Zionist vision by secular Jewry – in the face of opposition from religious Jewry – ensured that the culture of the new Jewish state would be, by and large, secular. From the nineteenth century on, secular Jewish culture spread to every corner of the Diaspora and into every Jewish and non-Jewish language in which Jews wrote – Hebrew, Ladino, Yiddish, English, French, Russian, Arabic, German and others.

This essentially secular culture had roots stretching back into every period of Jewish history. The literature, art, scholarship and philosophy of twentieth-century Jews clearly reveal the imprint of the Bible and biblical culture, as well as the mark of each subsequent era. We can detect influences from the Hellenistic-Byzantine period (both Rabbinical and Hellenizing), the Middle Ages (including the communities of North Africa, the Middle East and Southern Europe), and the Renaissance and Enlightenment (Haskalah).

Modern secular Jewry developed out of a profound reappraisal of that heritage. Literature, jurisprudence, the plastic arts and theology were reviewed in a revelatory new light. Once considered only a religious text, the Bible was rediscovered as an anthology of literature, historiography and law codes, mostly religiously inspired, but not always (as in the case of the Song of Songs and the Book of Esther). The sheer variety of form and content of this anthology, and the multiplicity of its beliefs and conceptions of God, bore witness to the pluralism of the Jewish world in its first thousand years, a pluralism that thousands of years later would, with equal force, inspire both secular and religious authors.

This new conception that Judaism is the pluralist, constantly evolving culture of the whole Jewish people, that the Jewish religion is a key component but far, far from the whole of it, is a radical departure. Judaism as a culture is represented in all forms and media of Jewish creativity, in all its streams and movements – secular and religious.

Jewish Studies taught in this light are not only very different from Judaism taught as a religion, but also very unlike Jewish political, social and economic history as they are generally taught. Although this new perception reflects the majority view, very few Jewish Studies programs have made it their point of departure in developing curricula.

FREEDOM OF CHOICE

Jews are not the "chosen people," as claimed by some religious circles: rather, they are a people who must apply choice to the way they realize both their Jewishness and their humanity. The issue of unavoidable choice confronts us in our children's education, in the style and content of our lives, and in our attitude to religious commandments. We have the freedom to choose whether to remain within the framework of traditional Judaism or move to another form, another paradigm, as did the majority of world Jewry during the late nineteenth and twentieth centuries.

The more Jews become aware of the variety of Judaisms and lifestyles within Jewry, and of the variety and span of Jewish creativity in every age of its history, the greater will be their freedom of choice and potential for contributing to the quality of their own cultural life.

As parent-educators, workers and social beings, every one of us has the creativity, and therefore the potential, to contribute to our culture and society. Parents assume responsibility for choosing how they will influence the course and content of their children's lives and how they will empower them to fulfil their unique potential as human beings and Jews. As our knowledge of Jewish and world culture expands, so does our capacity to enjoy their treasures and to play an active part in the cultural life of family and community. As our knowledge of Jewish and world culture expands, so does our freedom of choice.

LIBERATION FROM A RELIGION OF COMMANDMENTS

We have no obligation to obey the commandments. Even religiously believing Jews agree with that and take their authority from none other than Maimonides' *Guide for the Perplexed*. As early as the thirteenth century, some Jews decided they were free of the duty of *mitzva* observance. Their authority for this audacious conclusion was Maimonides' conceptualization of God as perfectly abstract and his likening of the practical commandments (*mitzvot*) to the custom of divine sacrifice. Maimonides had declared sacrifice no less than idolatry, a remnant of paganism it had taken centuries to eradicate. To a God abstract of all form or feature, it made no sense to ascribe the power of speech or a need for animal sacrifices or prayers. Only human nature, always reluctant to change, prevented abolishing the practice of sacrifice sooner.

To be liberated from commandments that seemed to be of no use and whose basis was unknown and unknowable made perfect sense to believers who perceived God as a reality that lay beyond any human ability to conceive. They could not accept the *mitzvot* as being of divine origin. Beyond their benefit to everyday life, which any person could judge for himself or herself, they were granted no validity. With every attempt to determine the grounds, purpose and justification of the *mitzvot*, the conviction strengthened that there was no duty to obey them. The outstanding investigatory efforts in this direction were those of Saadiah and Maimonides and their followers. Paradoxically, they led to two totally contradictory conclusions: (1) that there was no point in searching out grounds for the *mitzvot*, since their divine origin made them binding, hence the need to obey (school of Saadiah); and (2) that there was no point in obeying commands that originated in the human mind or whose purpose could not be fathomed (Jewish dissenters influenced by Maimonides' writings).

For contemporary Jews, the commandments and laws that pass the test of our fundamental values and generate real benefit to humankind should, of course, be "obeyed," especially those *mitzvot* that pertain to our dignity, freedom and equality. We are also free to create new *mitzvot*, such as those that support the precepts of democracy. Only obedience to these laws can sustain a society that expands people's humanity and raises their quality of life. Beneficial traditional practices, such as setting aside a Sabbath day for leisure – unrestricted by *Halakhic* prohibitions – or celebrating the life-enriching seasonal and historical festivals, deserve a place in our social and cultural life. On the other hand, commandments and customs that yield no visible benefit, or that are plainly discriminatory (especially to women) and in which the secular find no useful function, are better replaced. Examples include *Halakhic* prohibitions on the Sabbath, which prevent people from enjoying culture, social gatherings and outings on their day of leisure, or the Passover custom of reciting the traditional *Haggadah* – despite the boredom and incomprehension of most people at the table.

In sum, the notions of observing *mitzvot* and following traditional practices need to be examined and possibly replaced. Do they stand the test of fundamental humanistic values and visible benefit? The guiding principle is our duty to the laws of democracy and to those *mitzvot* that raise humanity to a higher level.

Many Jews who acknowledge Yahweh as man-made – as a figure created by literary texts, painting and sculpture – nonetheless keep the *mitzvot,* in the twin beliefs that they have a duty to respect ancestral traditions and that *mitzva* observance promotes the unity of the Jewish people. The *mitzvot* may mean nothing to any divinity, they say in effect, but they are nevertheless an asset to the Jews. Among freethinking Jews, there are those who believe, like the philosopher Baruch Spinoza, that the universe itself is divine and that divinity is inseparable from the natural reality around us. Others, like Martin Buber, experience God as the "thou" in the universe to whom their "I" speaks, or like Albert Einstein, as the awesomely complex but beautiful lawfulness that rules both the micro- and macro-cosmos.

Atheists, certain that it was man who has created all gods and "divine" commandments, neither keep "his *mitzvot*" nor pray to a man-made concept. In this they may draw support from the ancient prophets, who also denounced the cult of man-made gods. Agnostics (believing that the reality of God is unknowable and that his reality or unreality alters nothing in our lives) and Deists (who believe that God exists but, uninterested in us, has no hand in our world or our lives) also claim no obligation to those *mitzvot* devoid of spiritual or other advantage.

Common to these views is the confidence that the *mitzvot* were not "proclaimed" by the tongue or "written" by the hand of Yahweh, for Yahweh has no conceivable body or words. Whether one believes in a God of a kind beyond the conceptual powers of humankind to conceive or believes that Yahweh has been manufactured by the human imagination, the *mitzvot* lose their power to command obedience. In the eyes of both groups, the commandments are no more than customs, conventions or traditional behavior patterns, or indeed the inventions by which some people try to rule others by invoking the authority of the "words and will of God."

Maimonides was commonly thought to have declared that those non-Jews who so respected the divine that they kept what he calls the seven *mitzvot* binding on all "children of Noah" belonged to "the righteous of the world." On the other hand, Jews who kept these same *mitzvot* out of intellectual conviction or for reasons of conscience were not of the "righteous." Yaakov Levinger has demonstrated that this is a misconception based on a text deliberately falsified by having its final lines removed. The full text concludes with the statement that those who keep the *mitzvot* out of intellectual conviction or for reasons of conscience are not of the "righteous of the world; they belong, rather, to the wise of the world." In another context, Maimonides recounts a parable in which the righteous are permitted only to walk around the outside of the Lord's palace, while the wise men and the philosophers enter into the Presence itself. His approval of this parable leads us to infer that Maimonides did indeed value the wise over the righteous, that is, over those who keep the *mitzvot* merely out of obedience.

BETWEEN "NATION" AND "RELIGION": A HISTORICAL OVERVIEW OF RELIGION-LESS JEWISH NATIONALITY

It is vital that we distinguish between Jewish nationality and the Jewish religion (the code of *Halakhic mitzvot*). In doing so we shall be doing exactly as the Israelites did in biblical times.

The uniqueness of the Jews in the past lay in their fusion of religion and nationality. From Hellenistic times through the medieval period, Jewish nationality was expressed in terms of a national religion, with an overlap between a *religio* and a *natio.* It was a religion practiced only by Jews. In contrast, other peoples could maintain the distinction between religion and nationality. Many, for example, throughout history, could adopt Christianity without altering their collective, or national, identity.

This distinction between Jews and others did not characterize every period of history, however. In the biblical era, preceding Hellenism, there was no overlap between a Jew's religion and nationality, no fusion of the two concepts. The same is true in our modern era. In biblical times, most Israelites worshiped non-Israelite gods but were nevertheless considered part of the Israelite nation – by themselves, their prophets, the biblical chroniclers and their foreign neighbors. The Israelites' own religion was split between two rival cults and belief systems: one, attributed to Moses, worshipped an exclusive and abstract Yahweh; the other, attributed to his brother Aaron, worshiped a Yahweh represented by a sculpted calf and was celebrated in the two central Yahwist temples in the larger of the two kingdoms of the Jews, at Dan and Bet El.

The Yahwist prophets and biblical redactors showered the Jews of the time with coals of fire for the multiplicity of gods they followed. Their tirades are strong evidence of the religious pluralism of the age and the distinction between the nation and its religion. This was a distinction the prophets and redactors themselves drew, between a religion exclusive to the people of Israel and an Israelite nationality that embraces the twelve tribes of Israel plus assorted other peoples who had joined them.

In the words of the prophets, the people of Israel had broken its covenant with the God of Israel, had not kept his faith, had not kept faith with him, and had not respected his oneness. They did not, however, exclude these faithless ones from "the people of Israel."

By the Hellenistic period, the fissures in religious practice and belief had grown much deeper. The Hasmonean (Maccabean) revolt, triggered by the execution of a Jew who dared make a sacrifice to a Greek god, symbolized a now unbridgeable gulf stretching between rabbinical Judaism and Judaism open to Hellenic ways and ideas. The adherents of the open Judaism were cursed by the other side as "Hellenizers" (*mityavnim*).

We see the same sort of fracture in the mutual antipathies of the Sadducees, Pharisees and Essenes. The Sadducean priestly establishment rejected the validity of the Oral Law as an authentic voice of Judaism; the Pharisees and the sages of the Oral Law were reformers who denied the exclusive authority of the written Torah as upheld by the Sadducees and Karaites; the Essenes called for a plague on both their houses. Only from the point of view of a non-Jew could the Jewish religion have appeared to be a unitary belief system. Within the House of Israel, the gulfs of practice and principle were so wide that some saw themselves as "sons of light" waging war against the "sons of darkness," just as they do today.

In the Hellenistic period and the Middle Ages, for all the depth and venom of these internal fissures, Jews of all Jewry's Judaisms nonetheless regarded themselves and were regarded by others as Jews – a religion and a nation. At a later period, the Kabbalist mystics may have departed radically from the philosopher-rationalists; the messianics may have clashed furiously with their denouncers; Jews living under Islam and the Italian Renaissance may have actively embraced the non-Jewish society and civilization while in Eastern Europe Jews erected walls against a hostile outside world. They nonetheless all regarded themselves and were regarded by others as Jews.

Towards the end of the Middle Ages and the start of the Enlightenment (Haskalah), Jews and non-Jews began to acknowledge as Jewish nationals even those who had abandoned the religion, even those condemned as apostates. Jews (even those who ceased to regard the *Halakhic* faith and *mitzvot* as binding) found they could not deny their shared historical roots and their recognition of the Bible as foundation of the nation and its collective memory. This was the case, for example, of Jews who converted to Christianity in Spain and Portugal before their mass expulsion, as well as of many Sabbatean messianists and Haskalah Jews (*maskilim*) who defined themselves (and were accepted by others) as Jewish freethinkers.

It was, oddly, the new anti-semitism of fifteenth-century Spain that fixed in the European mind – and in the Jewish mind as well – the notion of two distinct concepts: Judaism-as-religion and Judaism-as-nationality. Spaniards at the time, who had been Christian for generations, reacted with hatred to the "new Christians" (Jewish converts), whom they saw rising rapidly into the upper echelons of society, the government, the free professions and even the Catholic religious establishment responsible for the Inquisition. Their furious resentment took the form of a murderous loathing for all Jews, *whatever religion they professed*, and the horrors of this loathing have characterized racist anti-semitism ever since, culminating in the antisemitic laws legislated by the Nazis and the European states occupied by (or collaborating with) the Nazis.

This new conception of Jewish nationality spread widely among Jews as well. The rise of European nationalist movements and the establishment of nation-states in the nineteenth century helped solidify the distinction between nationality and religion. What did German Reform Jews ask of their non-Jewish compatriots but to separate the two and be accepted as "Germans of the Mosaic faith"? Educated secular Jews defined themselves as non-religious Jews. Though Heine and Mahler, for example, may have converted to Christianity to bypass barriers to professional advancement, their society continued to regard them as Jews. After meeting the composer Mendelssohn, whose father had converted to Christianity but retained his Jewish name, Queen Victoria wrote of meeting "that little dark Jew."

The nineteenth-century emancipation of Jews that released them from their rabbinically ruled communities and education systems, the mass emigrations of the nineteenth and twentieth centuries, the disintegration of the Eastern European *shtetl* and the concentration of Jews in the great cities of Europe and the Americas, all accelerated the secularization of the four-fifths of world Jewry now living in Europe and the Americas. These events reinforced their conviction that they remained Jews even as they forgot their religion. Mass movements of Jewish nationalism, Zionist and anti-Zionist, fuelled this trend, stressing the historical-cultural heritage common to all Jews. Zionism went on to establish a new secular Jewish state – again, for *all* Jews – and so bring to a culmination the long divorce of Jewish national identity from Jewish religious identity.

The laws of the new Jewish state now give formal recognition to Jewishness unconnected to religious practice or profession. The key to this disconnection is the Law of Return, which gives the right of citizenship and residency in Israel to all Diaspora Jews on the basis of Jewish ancestry alone. To the majority of Israeli Jews, this acknowledgment of a shared history and fate and a unique language and culture is the most important part of their Jewishness.

An Israeli's identity as a Jew is no longer contingent on religious identity. The uniqueness of the Jewish people in our day and age is no longer defined by the Jewish religion. The great majority, after all, do not keep the *mitzvot* but accept the religion as part of the historical-cultural heritage to which all Jews are heir. They no longer accept it as a defining and compulsory lifestyle.

A CRITICAL RESPONSE TO THE "SOURCES OF JUDAISM"

It is vital that we respond to the sources of Judaism, the heritage of its texts from the Bible to modern Hebrew literature, both intellectually and emotionally. Secular Jews have not the least intention of abandoning or undermining their bond to their own cultural heritage. The curriculum of Jewish secular education, the products of modern secular culture and the creative effort the secular invest in celebrating the Jewish festivals all attest to the veracity of this statement.

The restoration of Hebrew as the spoken and written vernacular of Israeli Jews afforded them unmediated access to the classics of their national literature.

In secular Jewish culture, the Bible replaced the Talmud, which the Orthodox had made the near totality of Jewish education. The new approach to this ancient compendium displayed a sense of objectivity in searching out its sources and tracing its link and debt to the texts and cultures of neighboring civilizations.

Modern literary criticism inspired the idea of reading the books of the Bible as works of literature. The stories were linked with the latest archaeological discoveries and historical research. The Bible and other venerable texts were given new life; readers were encouraged to experience the Bible's poetry and emotionality, without having to suspend their rational and analytic powers. The outcome was a deeper and more intimate bond between reader and text.

The degree to which schools expose children to the excitement of books, paintings and other arts will manifest itself in the richness of their spiritual world as adults. In the latter half of the twentieth century, some education systems succumbed to an approach that erected barriers between reader and text and drove most students away from literature as a field of study. While textual criticism may be necessary for historical research, it is the literary-experiential approach that enriches the spirit.

A NEW APPROACH TO JEWISH HISTORY

The writing of critical Jewish history by Jews did not really begin until the nineteenth century. With a few exceptions since Josephus, the past two thousand years have, historiographically speaking, stood still. Secular historians do not view history as the unfolding of God's will: they assess sequences, episodes, events, behaviors and products that, from the vantage point of the historian's own period, can be knitted into meaningful trends and developments. This is not the religious view.

For the ancient prophets and religion-inspired thinkers who followed in their footsteps, the history of the Jewish people is the history of its relationship with Yahweh, the God who had chosen them from among all other peoples. The schema of this history is supposed to have been known in advance. Starting with the mythic covenant sealed between Yahweh and Israel, it proceeds to the devastation and exile wreaked on the people as punishment for violating that covenant. This is a punishment – for their sins and those of their forefathers – that they are required to endure in patient suffering, until Yahweh, in customary wilful and arbitrary style, sees fit to dispatch his redeeming messiah and return the Jews to their lost homeland.

Secular historians of Judaism have a different perspective. Anti-semitism in all its forms and manifestations, which the religious consider both a component of divine punishment and a major factor in Jewish history, is viewed as a form of racist pathology. It afflicts peoples all over the world, taking its particular form according to the religious teaching – Christian, Muslim or other – onto which it is grafted.

Even before Christianity arrived on the scene, pagan writers in the Hellenistic period responded to the strangeness and peculiarities of the Jewish religion with an early form of anti-semitism. Jewish monotheism and the refusal to accord equal respect to other peoples' gods were perceived as a form of atheism, their Sabbath as laziness, their practice of circumcision as barbaric. On the other hand, the source of Christian anti-Judaism was kinship: the new religion was competing with the old for "intellectual rights" to the same body of scripture and for the allegiance of the same followers.

One hundred and fifty years after the French Revolution and the emancipation of the Jews, anti-semitism was taken up by two secular regimes (the Soviet Union and Nazi Germany) and reached a culmination in the Holocaust, the annihilation of the Jewish people. Within religious Jewry, many saw the Holocaust as another example of divine penalty for the nation's sins, especially for the sin of Zionist hubris – i.e., for refusing to wait for the Messiah and presuming to bring about national redemption by human agents.

The Holocaust made anti-semitism the pre-eminent symbol of murderous racism in all its manifestations, the paradigm of how society is destroyed when taken over by the leaders of a mass movement rooted in the hatred of one ethnic group for another.

The European manifestation of anti-semitism spread its germs to the Middle East, where *The Protocols of the Elders of Zion* enjoys a lively circulation to this very day. Forged by Tsarist police agents in the early twentieth century and given the stamp of authenticity a decade later by *The Times* of London, this description of the Jewish conspiracy to control the world is still given credence in some Arab countries.

To present anti-semitism as a dominant factor in the development of Jewry since the destruction of the Second Temple is misleading. Jewish culture should not be seen strictly through the prism of anti-semitism but should be known through its works and ideas. The emphasis on anti-semitism and the study of the *Shoah* (Holocaust), important as they are, tend to hide from students the fact that Jewish history is enmeshed with the political and social developments of other peoples. Jewish social structures took shape in the context of this history, as did religious and ideological movements and schools of philosophy.

Zionism offered Jews the solution to their years of persecution in the Diaspora. No longer does Jewish history need or deserve to be recounted only as a history of persecution or as the tale of Yahweh's savage wrath visited on twentieth-century Jews for the sins of their biblical ancestors. The fundamental change needed in our appraisal of Jewish history is even more urgent in our approach to Holocaust studies, for the Holocaust, in the understanding of many Jews and non-Jews, has come to represent and typify the whole of Jewish history.

A NEW APPROACH TO HOLOCAUST STUDIES

Teaching the Holocaust as a litany of murder and physical destruction, without teaching the Jewish culture and society that were destroyed, is to give students a distorted picture of European Jewry in the modern period. In high schools, colleges and universities around the world, Holocaust Studies are considered not merely a segment of twentieth-century Jewish history, but of its epitome. This one-dimensional focus totally ignores the richness of Jewish culture and achievement in a century that witnessed Jewry's greatest creative output in 3,000 years (in its volume, variety of subject matter and geographical range).

The Holocaust was a culmination of the historical development of anti-semitism and represents the worst trauma ever suffered by the Jewish people. As such, it must be studied and it merits a special place in the history of twentieth-century Jewry. However, teaching it only as a history of physical murder and destruction without teaching the Jewish culture and society that were destroyed is to give students a distorted picture. European Jewry is depicted as moving straight from the decaying hovels of the nineteenth-century *shtetl* to Auschwitz. The story of the enormous cultural and secular outpouring that energized all sectors of Jewry in Europe in the nineteenth and first half of the twentieth centuries goes untold and is an unforgivable violation against those who were murdered.

The Holocaust cut down European Jewish civilization at one of the triumphal peaks of its development. Jews were working, producing and innovating in all Jewish and non-Jewish languages, in the sciences, commerce and the arts, in the great socio-political movements of the day, and in scholarship and journalism. The background and catalyst to this surge in energy and vision was the secularization of the late nineteenth and early twentieth centuries, when large numbers of Jews moved from the *shtetl* into the capitals of Europe. To ignore this fact is to do historical injustice to the victims of the Holocaust and the spiritual-intellectual world they created.

The greater part of this cultural outpouring reflects the revolutionary changes that, by the twentieth century, had transformed the face of Jewish society. The productivity in the arts, scholarship and science – in the form of novels, essays, films, stage plays, historiography or atomic research – represents a secular response to Judaism and human life in general. The great majority of Jewish creative minds found their niche in Western civilization, and many made a decisive impact in their fields.

Holocaust Studies must, therefore, be reshaped by a new approach. The Holocaust should be taught as an essential element in the evolution of the whole Jewish people and its civilization, a horrific event that played out in the context of political and socio-cultural developments in European Jewry and its host nations.

JUDAISM, JEWRY, AND DEMOCRACY

Contrary to narrow orthodox perspectives, ever since the sages of the Talmud legitimized analysis of ideas by open controversy and decision by majority, democratic and humanistic principles have had the upper hand in the Jewish world. Hillel the Elder formulated the core principle of ethics when he gave his famous reply to the pagan's question "What is the gist of the Torah?" "Do not do to others what you would hate done to you" was his answer, encapsulating the ethical essence of the Ten Commandments in the spirit of the prophets' demand for the priority of social justice over religious ritual. With these words, Hillel laid down for all time the essence of Torah as ethical, humanist and universal.

Hillel's formulation, less ambiguous than impossible requirements such as "Love thy neighbor as thyself," is at one with the humanist moral precepts formulated much later by Kant and acknowledged by the open society of Western Europe. Judaism's humanistic values are actually universal values in Jewish garb. Admittedly, numerous Jews and Jewish societies have preached and practiced anti-humanism. Some national leaders, as represented by the books of Deuteronomy and Joshua, even sanctioned genocide. But most Jewish communities today, both secular and religious, conduct themselves, their education and their politics in accordance with a democratic humanist code.

Humanist democratic values, it is worth reiterating, proceed from the premise that they are created by men and women for the benefit of humanity. This premise is true even if the values are believed to have come from the mouth of God, as this belief is also a product of the human mind.

What was the purpose of the great sages who carried through a reform of Judaism by drawing up the Oral Law if not to adjust and adapt Judaism to changed circumstances? The Talmud states explicitly that their object was to formulate *Halakhot* (rulings), which would serve a people experiencing a changing reality. Having come to the conclusion that no man or woman any longer commanded the authority to speak in the name of God, the sages understood that the only way to lay down a ruling in cases of unresolved controversy, without breaking up Jewish society, was to leave the decision to majority vote. Minority opinion was carefully preserved, however. Rabbi Yehuda, for example, proclaimed that with the passage of time, minority opinions might be adopted by the majority.

The culture of open debate, apparent in much of the Talmud, is a legacy that needs to be retained and remembered. These guiding principles – that law-making must address people's needs and welfare, and that verdicts are best reached by majority decision (rather than by obedience to an individual who presumes to speak for God) – are also an essential part of democratic humanism. The well-known dispute over the "kosherness" of Akhnai's oven is the epitome of this phenomenon: although the voice of heaven is heard in support of the minority opinion against the earthly sages, it was finally admitted that even the God of Israel is overruled by a majority of his mortal judges.

The history of Judaism is riddled with battles between the forces of humanism and antihumanism, between democracy and arbitrary rule. Attempts to improve the status of women in the patriarchal family (Rabbi Gershom's prohibition of polygamy, for instance, a revolutionary reversal of *Halakha*) were met by the obstinate efforts of other *Halakhic* authorities (all men, of course) to keep women subjugated (even in cases where the woman was the breadwinner and sole supporter of her husband). Pressure to institute democratic processes, including elections, in the administration of community and public bodies was met by the intransigence of Orthodox rabbis and wealthy notables who, preferring their own oligarchy, insisted that all community agents and activists continue to obey the rabbi, with no possibility of higher appeal.

By the end of the twentieth century, democracy had swept away its opponents in most spheres of Jewish life around the globe. The new Jewish state was established on democratic and secular foundations, and its body of law includes Fundamental (Constitutional) Laws enshrining humanist values.

Elected leadership runs most Jewish communities in the world, and rabbis have no power to impose their will on the majority. Today, most Jewish schools and colleges espouse democratic humanist principles, and only small minorities of ultra-Orthodox movements still impart chauvinistic and even racist ideology.

The victory of democracy in the Jewish world is symbolized by the fact that, in Israel, the law of the state prevails in all cases where secular state law clashes with the *Halakhic* law practiced by the rabbinical courts.

DEMOCRACY AND JEWISH EDUCATIONAL METHODS

In the vast Babylonian Jewish community, it was customary for men to be members of an informal but lifelong Torah and Talmud study group (*limud matmid*), and it was in these groups that a method of study by textual analysis came into general use. All questions were hammered out in open debate. The practice was developed and perfected in centuries that followed.

We are currently in the process of rediscovering the educational value and effectiveness of close textual analysis in small groups. It works, of course, only on condition that certain aspects of the text be not set aside as divine attributes and, as such, become unquestionable. It is a method that encourages questioning, refutation and the dissection of rival interpretations. It demands a critical facility, the ability to marshal thoughts cogently and the mastery of several languages. It develops the skills needed for the cut and thrust of debate – pointed analysis, strong arguments and command of multiple sources. More importantly, the essence of the method – controlled dispute as a means of approaching the truth – has been one of the key factors promoting democracy to its dominant position in Judaism today. It was by promoting unity without uniformity, thrashing out controversies while maintaining peaceful coexistence and settling dispute by majority vote, that Jewry sustained its development.

The same methods are still in use in most denominations of Judaism, both secular and religious: all the traditions, conventions and *Halakhot* we have inherited are subjected to criticism and debate. The principle of "you shall not follow a multitude to do evil" has also helped sustain the culture of debate, both in Israel and the Diaspora.

The opposition to the supremacy of democratic values in cases of conflict between *Halakha* and the civil law comes from religious Jewry's Orthodox minority. The representatives of the ultra-Orthodox political parties in the Knesset and Local Government Authorities in Israel are appointed by rabbis, not elected. As might be expected, when democratically legislated statutes clash with rabbinical rulings, these representatives fervently defend *Halakha* and denounce the law.

Democracy is the best means of guaranteeing that humanist values rule our society. Its norms are clearly well suited to this end – equality of rights and obligations; equality of opportunity; universal right of choice; the state's right to enforce its democratically-made laws and the rulings of its judicial system; the protection of every population group from persecution, oppression and discrimination; and the separation of legislative, executive and judiciary powers.

In the *Halakha*-versus-state dispute there can be no "compromise," since both draw on entirely different orders of authority. Of course, there can and ought to be dialogue in order to promote mutual understanding and increase the chances of peaceful coexistence. This dialogue has been successfully achieved in France, Britain and the US, where there are sizeable Jewish communities that live peacefully within a democratic framework. Paradoxically, this sort of dialogue has been less successful in Israel.

CHAPTER 7

PLURALISM: A GUIDING PRINCIPLE AND SALIENT CHARACTERISTIC OF JUDAISM

PLURALISM AT THE CORE OF JUDAISM

Three thousand worshipers of Yahweh (in the form of a golden calf) were killed by the soldiers of Moses in a single day. This famous episode in the desert, following the Exodus from Egypt and the descent of Moses from Mount Sinai, opens the history of the long-running struggle for pluralism in Judaism.

Two schools of thought fought to the death over whether God was to take on a form, in this case the form of a calf, or was to be conceived as an abstract entity that had named himself "I shall be what I shall be." Also at issue was the form of his cult: either the offering of sacrifices in a temple-sanctuary flanked by two great carved statues of *kheruvim*, or individual unmediated communion with him in the Tent of Meeting.

A few hundred years later, we find the same schools of religious thought in collision once again. In Israel's two ancient temples in the larger of the two kingdoms, Yahweh was worshipped in the form of a sculpted calf, while at the new temple in Jerusalem he was venerated in the abstract – he was represented in the Holy of Holies by the Ark of the Covenant, installed, once again, under the wings of the *kheruvim*.

Even before the Israelites settled in Canaan, they had taken up with Canaanite gods. That, of course, did not make them any less "Israelite," in spite of their slanted portrayal in the books of the Bible. From then on, in both kingdoms and until the Babylonian exile, their religious culture may be termed pluralistic: Yahwist monotheism had to compete with a multiplicity of other gods and cults. Solomon erected his glorious temple to Yahweh in Jerusalem;

yet he also built temples to many other gods. "On every hill ... and under every green tree," said the prophets, stood an altar to Ba'al or Ashtoreth. Even the great Temple to Yahweh in Jerusalem housed, for two-thirds of the time it stood, a statue of Asherah, mother of the Canaanite pantheon. Though the prophets and the editors of the Bible may have denounced this religious promiscuity, they also recognized it as rooted in the Israelite way of life ever since their arrival in Canaan.

In the Hellenistic period, pluralism assumed new forms and dimensions. Jews were split between rabbinical and Hellenizing Judaism. The followers of the great rabbis labelled their opposition *mityavnim* ("Hellenizers") – precisely the derogatory term applied today by the ultra-Orthodox to the majority of the Jewish People. Another faultline in religious theory and practice ran between the Sadducees (conservative and dominant in the establishment) and the Pharisees (reformers and authors of the Oral Law). Other sects – Essenes, Baptizers, Hassidim, Judeo-Christians, and Zealots – made the mosaic even more complex.

Once again religious-cultural disputes triggered civil war. The Maccabee-led war of liberation from Syrian-Hellenic religious coercion had a second dimension of Jew versus Jew. Years after that war brought about a newly autonomous Jewish kingdom, civil war broke out again when the Pharisees rose up against King Alexander Yannai, who in their eyes was imitating Hellenistic ways.

This embittered divide between Hellenizing and rabbinical Judaism, which was evident both in the Land of Israel and in the Diaspora, is a salient characteristic of pluralism of the period. It manifested itself in all aspects of lifestyle, art and scholarship. In education, the yeshiva opposed the *gymnasia.* In literature and scholarship, Talmudic, Midrashic and mystic interpretations were in conflict with the *pshatt,* literal interpretation, as in the Greek translation of the Bible.

In Hellenized Jewry, philosophy, historiography, poetry and drama flourished, and all were written in Greek. Greek mosaics and frescoes also influenced a range of Jewish creativity, evidenced on the walls and floors of synagogues and homes.

An amazing range of works composed by Jews in the last centuries BCE and the first centuries CE demonstrates the richness and variety of Judaism at the time. Besides the works included in the then canonized Bible, scores of famous literary works were created, among them the Apocrypha, the New Testament, the Books of the Maccabees and the works of Philo of Alexandria and Josephus Flavius.

The Talmud and its commentators ignored this Jewish Hellenized literature, including some of its most influential output, such as the New Testament, which traced the thinking and development of a sect formed by the disciples of Rav Yeshua (Jesus) of Nazareth, who they believed was the promised Messiah. The Dead Sea Scrolls introduce us to the apocalyptic thinking of another sect that had withdrawn from mainstream Judaism. To all these, we must add what has already been mentioned in passing: the Septuagint translation of the Bible, the philosophy and history-writing of Philo and Josephus, the work of Ezekiel the Dramatist, and novelists and poets writing in Greek in the (perhaps one-million-strong) Egyptian Jewish community and elsewhere in North Africa.

The Middle Ages saw Jewry's gradual fragmentation into geographical-cultural communities scattered among diverse Christian and Muslim host cultures in North Africa, the Middle East and Europe. Rationalist trends (exemplified by the writings of Saadiah, Maimonides and their disciples) stretched further and further away from the forces of mysticism – from Yitzhak the Blind in Provence, through Nakhmanides in Gerona and the literature of the Zohar, to the Lurian School in Safad.

When Maimonides' books were publicly burned in France in the thirteenth century, it was only too evident how strong Jewry's centrifugal forces had become. Internal enmities worsened when Sabbateanism and its Frankist offshoots stoked the messianist and nationalist fires, and the gap between Jewish religion and Jewish nationality began to widen.

The differences in lifestyle, synagogue liturgy and customs of Ashkenazis (in Eastern Europe), Sephardis (in Western Europe and around the Mediterranean), and other geographically separated communities (in Central Asia, Yemen, Abyssinia and even distant China) widened significantly during the Middle Ages.

During the Renaissance and the Enlightenment, these centrifugal trends became even stronger. Evidence is abundant: the spread of Hassidism in Eastern Europe and the furious opposition to it (led by the Vilna Gaon); the rise of *Haskalah* (Jewish Enlightenment) movements in Italy and Western Europe (from Spinoza to Felix Mendelssohn, Hermann Cohen and Martin Buber); the spread of the *Haskalah* and secularization into Eastern Europe with the flowering of secular Jewish writing in Yiddish, Hebrew, German and other European languages.

In the Islamic world, too, European culture and languages were adopted by circles of Jewish intellectuals in most of the large Jewish communities. The network of schools built by the Alliance Israélite encouraged the trend. In the nineteenth and twentieth centuries the ethno-geographical and ideological divisions between religious and secular Jews widened still further as secularization and mass emigration carried each other forward and the centers of gravity of world Jewry moved to Western Europe, the Americas and Palestine. Orthodox-religious and secular Jews continued to drift apart in their lifestyles, festivals celebrations, adherence to *mitzvot*, attitudes towards nationalism and democracy, spoken and read languages, and relationships with non-Jewish cultures.

Over the course of the twentieth century, the majority of the world's Jews abandoned Orthodoxy and its *Halakha*, leaving behind a shrinking Orthodox community that continually attempted to ensure its survival by entrenching itself in extremist positions. Orthodoxy fortifies itself behind Hatam Sofer's (early-nineteenth-century) dictum that "The Torah forbids innovation," an antipluralist remark that recalls similar attempts in Jewish history to arrest the development of Judaism. The Sadducees, Samaritans and Karaites all attempted to arrest change, and all three dwindled away until they were no longer a factor in Judaism.

UNITY OR UNIFORMITY?

In the non-uniformity of the Diaspora, many "Judaisms" live side by side: Reform, Conservative, Secular, Reconstructionist, New Age, Orthodox, and others. Israel today is an arena where all currents in Judaism meet. Because of their economic, military and political interdependence, however, the friction between them is aggravated. It is only too obvious that without pluralism and the acceptance of non-uniformity there will be no unity, as the unity of most peoples presupposes a plurality of political ideologies and parties.

Jewish unity has never taken the form of uniformity. Unity has resided in Jews' persistence in seeing themselves as one people. "Normative Judaism" has always been a title that Jews of one sect or movement have bestowed on themselves in order to portray the others as deviant. The founding and establishment of the State of Israel and the stream of immigration it attracted from every stream and community of Judaism has been one of the most impressive expressions of that unity.

Developments in the nineteenth and twentieth centuries demonstrated that Jews could change denominations, or switch from one ideological movement to another, without abandoning their Jewish identity. They could retain their Jewish nationality even as they adopted new positions regarding the *Halakha*, *mitzvot*, festivals, the Messiah and every other component of Judaism.

One of the virtues of pluralism, as deeply rooted in the present as in the past, is that it allows Jews to remain Jews even after they have abandoned ultra-Orthodoxy for secularism. Over the last 150 years, the shift of the majority of world Jewry from one kind of Judaism to another has created a new, varied map of their culture. Jews now choose the type of Jewish faith they adhere to: atheist, agnostic, pantheist, deist, mystical or traditional. Pluralism and the permanent state of dispute between Jewry's sects and movements have never been anything but beneficial for both the volume and variety of Jewish cultural productivity. The thousands of new works created in the twentieth century gave new life, form and energy to Judaism of all types.

PLURALISM – A GUIDING PRINCIPLE

From Talmudic times on, Judaism has encouraged the clash of opinion and belief: the Talmudic expression "Both these and these are the living words of God" conveys faith in the many faces of Truth.

Amid constricting Orthodox views, also present these days, multiplicity of opinion and belief has been an explicitly legitimate approach to Judaism, as well as a proven catalyst of cultural-intellectual advancement and innovation. In fact, the Talmud elevated this multiplicity into a guiding principle. It was the sages of the Talmud who cultivated and established a culture of dialogue and controversy. Though Classical Greek culture may have been their inspiration, the sages translated it into something original and unique to Judaism.

The dictum "Both these and these are the living words of God" expresses the conviction that only through dispute and debate is it possible to approach Truth. Open dispute and debate – a salient feature of Talmudic texts – forces participants to examine their underlying assumptions, postulates and ethical values. Dialogue between conflicting opinions clarifies the possible conclusions of each party's argument, and these conclusions can be later used to evaluate those arguments.

This complex and cumulative process of analysis and debate increases the chances of discovering new truths, even when the parties reach no agreement and the issue must be settled by majority decision. The principle of the legitimacy of controversy is accepted today as a condition of an open, democratic society.

The Talmudic culture of debate, to which secular Judaism owes a significant debt, appears as a novelty in comparison with the authoritarian image of the Bible. Beginning with Moses and continuing with the prophets, the Word of God was a "revelation": the prophet either spoke directly with Yahweh or saw him in a vision or a dream and thus could speak in his name. Revealed prophecies and instructions thus demanded obedience, leaving little room for open debate. Moses settled the first theological controversy by force, first setting armed men against the worshipers of the Golden Calf, and then ordering the factionist Korakh and his followers to be buried alive. When King Ahab and his court adopted the cult of Ba'al and Ashtoreth, the Yahwist prophets had to flee for their lives and hide in desert caves, whereupon Elijah turned the tables by inciting a mob to massacre the Ba'alist prophets.

It was during the Talmudic period, when prophets were no longer recognized, that the idea of controversy became legitimate. The sages acknowledged that each of them was voicing his own opinion and was not speaking in God's name. In the dialogue-based literature that developed during the Hellenistic period (the

Book of Job an early forerunner), the participants acknowledge that every opinion contributing to a debate is legitimate and that none of them contains the whole truth. "The Torah has seventy faces," as the Talmudic saying illustrates. It was the long-running, and frequently heated, duel of judgement between the schools of Hillel and Shammai that gave rise to the famous dictum that "Both these and these are the living words of God."

As men of deep faith, most of the rabbis whose arguments and rulings are quoted in the Talmud believed that human wrangling found its eventual resolution only in Yahweh's infinite wisdom, where all views fused into an indivisible divine truth, a comprehensive vision beyond the grasp of man's finite intelligence. The truths revealed to human minds were inevitably partial. Thus came another significant Talmudic innovation: the recognition that some disputes needed to remain unresolved "until the coming of the Messiah." The term used, *T-Y-K-U*, is an acronym signifying, perhaps, "stalemate." Compromise and openly accepted indecision thus entered the field of Jewish theology. Not every problem has a human solution.

The method of analysis and debate practiced by the Talmudic sages was perpetuated by the generations that followed. It is a method that precludes blind obedience to authority and the rote learning of dogma and articles of faith. The method also views Jewish thought as a never-ending process that *Halakha* constantly develops, and it permits rival ideas and opinions always to exist side by side. Together, these two Talmudic principles – the virtue of open controversy and debate and the need to recognize that some issues cannot be brought to an agreed-upon conclusion – amounted to an acceptance of a plural society, a principle that remains unrecognized in some ossified, Orthodox circles.

MAJORITY RULINGS – NECESSARY BUT TEMPORARY

A dispute that cannot be resolved by agreement or compromise can be left "to be settled by the Messiah" only so long as practical realities do not demand a resolution. However, when laws have to be passed or judicial trials brought to a verdict, there is no substitute for majority vote.

The Talmudic episode of "Akhnai's Oven" indicates how, even when a voice from Heaven interferes to settle the debate, a majority of rabbis can overrule it. When a decision is crucial, there is no alternative to majority vote, even if it later turns out to have been wrong or only temporary. Rabbi Yehuda warned that the minority opinion must be formally stated and recorded since a majority decision will stand only as long as the majority behind it does. Even if the composition of the panel of judges or legislators does not change, new majority thinking can emerge with time.

A majority ruling is therefore not the terminus of any dispute but only a station on the way. This introduction of the temporal criterion legitimates the reopening of controversies after some time. It also legitimates a constant review of the body of *Halakha* and permits sweeping changes in it from time to time. Avi Saguy's book, *Both These and These,* analyzes the importance of pluralism as a guiding principle in Judaism and the function it has fulfilled through the generations in the evolution and development of religious thought.

It is a principle that, having originated in religious Jewry, is alive and strong in modern secular Jewry and in the legislative and judicial branches of the democratic Jewish State. In the final analysis, this is the best answer to the charge that Judaism and democracy are incompatible.

It was the theory and practice of pluralism that enabled the sages living and working from about 300 BCE to 500 CE to carry through major *Halakhic* reform, called the Oral Law. It was the same theory and practice that in the nineteenth century enabled a *Halakhic* code (whose development the relatively new Orthodox movement had striven to halt) to be revised once more by reform movements.

Today, as a consequence of such changes, Reform and Conservative Judaism have become the religion of the majority of religious Jewry the world over. A parallel reform process is currently under way in Israel. Under its democratic system of government, all laws, both religious and secular, are under constant review by parliament and the courts, both of which respect majority rule. This willingness to modify or nullify outdated laws is seen as a serious threat by a group that aspires to elevate *Halakha* into a body of dogma that defines and obligates all Jews.

As we have seen, it was precisely the abandonment of the principle of pluralism and reform by extremist Orthodoxy that helped secularization gain ground so rapidly in the nineteenth century.

There is no escaping the conclusion, therefore, that secular Judaism, together with various reform movements in religious Judaism, are the true "traditionalists." The Hebrew root of the word *Halakha* is a word signifying "walking," i.e., changing, just as the English "tradition" comes from the Latin *tradere,* "to hand over, to pass on." Tradition signifies change, not solidification.

CHAPTER 8

JUDAISM FROM A SECULAR PERSPECTIVE – AN EDUCATIONAL PROGRAM

A HUMANIST EDUCATION IN PLURALIST JUDAISM

While a humanist education is implanted in a national culture, the values it attempts to instil are universal. Many of the core values of humanism are part of Judaism's central ethical tradition (the Ten Commandments, the prophets' exhortations to social justice, Hillel's master-values); however, most *Halakhic* rules cannot be considered ethical values, and secular Judaism does not acknowledge all *mitzvot* as "Jewish values." Thinking men and women constantly face the challenge of re-evaluating their values and finding ways to practice them within the realities of family and community life.

Secular humanist Judaism teaches Jewish studies from its own point of view, as do all other Judaisms. Its ultimate goal is to give students an appreciation and understanding of Jewry's past and present civilization, beliefs, customs, laws (religious and secular), arts and scholarship. To attain this goal, one would need to experience the emotional-spiritual force of the cultural heritage, while internalizing its expressions of universal values.

Judaism should be taught as a culture, which, like all cultures, includes religion as one of its components. The "sources of Judaism" go beyond biblical, Talmudic and other religious literature to include the outstanding and characteristic creations of every Judaism and ethnic community in Jewry throughout history.

Historians, archaeologists, linguists, ethnographers, authors and literary critics have reassessed and transformed our understanding of Jewry's past and our reading of its works. Some works – the Apocrypha, the Books of the Maccabees, Philo, Josephus, the New Testament, the Dead Sea Scrolls and secular poetry – have been restored to Jewish culture. After centuries of oblivion, the banished classics of Jewish culture need to form a part of a Jewish humanistic education.

JUDAISM AS CULTURE – AN INTERDISCIPLINARY STUDY PROGRAM

The content of the program spans Jewish civilization and culture – its social institutions and lifestyles, politics and commerce, literature and arts, liturgy, the synagogue's social and religious functions, the festival calendar and more.

The study of Judaism as culture will combine interdisciplinary surveys of a historical era with the study of works representing the different trends and movements in Judaism during that period. In the same way that the Bible anthologizes a thousand years of Israelite/Jewish oral and written culture, we must compose anthologies for all other eras of Jewish history, each presenting Jewish culture in every media, genre, language and geographical region.

GUIDING PRINCIPLES

1. The present as a starting point

Judaism to be approached first as the culture of the Jewish People in the twentieth and the twenty-first centuries, including its sources over the past thirty centuries and focusing on the changes and developments in Jewish culture in ancient Israel and the Diaspora.

The interdisciplinary study of Judaism as culture will include descriptive and critical surveys of works of literature, the plastic and performing arts, religious and secular beliefs and lifestyles, ideology and philosophy representative of each era in the development of Jewish culture.

2. Judaism as the culture of the Jewish People in the biblical era

The Bible, as the basis of Judaism and the only cultural common denominator of all secular and religious Judaisms, will be studied as the classical literature of the Jewish People and as an anthology of religious and historical documents.

The biblical works of literature represent the pluralistic culture of the Jewish People in the first millennium BCE, their religious beliefs and practices, the ethical monotheism of the prophets and its clash with their opponents, the role of legal systems, the role of figurative art in biblical Judaism, and the distinction between national and religious identity (since the ancient Israelites worshipped numerous gods while maintaining their Israelite identity).

Works of literature in the Bible will be approached from aesthetic and ethical points of view, separate from the study of the historical evidence they present. The *pshatt* interpretation of the Hebrew text (the meaning of words and phrases according to their use of Hebrew as a spoken and written language) will enable the reader to enjoy the literary works in the Bible as they do other classical works of literature, such as those by Shakespeare or Goethe. The first most important work in *pshatt* interpretation of the Bible was performed by Jewish scholars in Egypt in the beginning of the Hellenistic era. The Greek translation of the Bible, the Septuagint, was intended for use by the hundreds of thousands of Jews who lived in Egypt at the time. The *pshatt* method of interpretation was joined by many religious *Midrashic* interpretations of the Bible – creative, imaginative readings of texts that became a leading literary form in Jewish culture.

3. *Judaism as the culture of the Jewish People in the Hellenistic-Byzantine era*

The pluralistic character of the culture of the Jewish People from the third century BCE to the seventh century CE is represented in a great variety of works of Jewish literature, historiography, philosophy and art. They include the Mishna, the Apocrypha, the works of Philo and Flavius, the two versions of the Talmud, the New Testament, Midrashic literature, figurative synagogue mosaics, the frescoes of Dura Europos, dramatic works for the theatre (such as "Exodus from Egypt" by Yecheskel of Cyrenaika-Lybia), mystical literature (such as *Sefer Yaytzsira* (the Book of Creation) and *Sheur Koma* (the description of the body of God as much bigger than the universe) and the literature of *Merkava* (chariots) and *Heihaloth* (palaces) describing the travels of Rabbi Akiva and Rabbi Ishmael to the world beyond and their meetings with thousands of angels and the Viceroy of God, "Metatron."

A study of the culture and history of ideas of the Jewish People must relate to this variety of sources and sectors within the Jewish nation and cannot limit itself to the study of the Talmudic and Midrashic literature (considered by religious orthodox thinkers as the sole representatives of post-biblical Judaism).

4. *Judaism as the culture of the Jewish People in the Middle Ages*

During the Middle Ages – from the Muslim conquests to the Renaissance – the Jewish People became increasingly fragmented, spreading to Asia, Africa and Europe and living under Christian and Islamic rule. The cultural distance between Jewish communities grew in spite of the unifying force of one religion and its basic rituals and rules.

In Jewish autonomous cultures and geographical centres, different ethnic groups were formed, speaking a variety of languages, Jewish and other – Yiddish in Eastern Europe, Ladino in northern Mediterranean regions, Jewish dialects of Arabic in North Africa and Yemen.

A wide range of beliefs and philosophical ideas were expressed in hundreds of works of literature, philosophical and religious treatises, interpretations of the Bible, poetry and prayers. The rational trends of philosophers such as Saadia and Maimonides clashed with mystical approaches of the Yehuda Chasid sect in Germany, Yitzhak the Blind in Provence, Nachmanides in Gerona and the authors of the basic book of the *Kabala*, the million-word anthology called the *Zohar*.

Jews were active in many scientific and other professional secular fields, such as medicine and medical education at universities, geography and cartography, philology and secular poetry, painting and the creation of manuscripts, architecture and building, crafts, finance and international commerce.

The autonomy of synagogues and their communities encouraged the development of diverse religious and ideological movements, as well as great differences in lifestyles and ways of celebrating holidays and life cycle ceremonies. Each ethnic-cultural community within the Jewish People – from Central Asia to India, Abyssinia, Poland, Turkey and North Africa – developed its own Jewish culture.

The study of Judaism in the Middle Ages will include works that describe and illustrate all the above-mentioned subjects, as well as the migrations of Jews from Western Europe to the East as a result of persecutions, pogroms and the expulsion of the Jewish population from settlements in which they had lived since the Roman Empire.

The birth of racial anti-semitism (in fifteenth-century Spain), which targeted Jews regardless of their stated religion, encouraged Messianic Jewish movements towards the end of the Middle Ages, and with it the beginning of a new national Jewish self-consciousness.

5. *The study of the Jewish People from the Enlightenment to the present*

The Jewish enlightenment movements were influenced by the Renaissance, the development of Humanism and national secular movements in Europe. The secularization process in Judaism started in Europe in the eighteenth century, shaped by the ideas of Spinoza in the previous century.

Almost simultaneously with the Enlightenment, the Chasidic movement was founded in the eighteenth century, and with it the religious orthodox movement. The clash between these two opposing trends in Judaism – secularization versus Orthodoxy – has left its imprint on Jewish social, political and cultural life in the past three hundred years.

The study of Jewish culture in the modern era will acquaint the student with a selection of contemporary expressions of this culture in all fields of Jewish creativity – literature, the arts, philosophy, ideologies, religious and secular movements and their enterprises (such as Jewish institutions and educational networks in the Diaspora and in Israel), and the State of Israel and its influence on Jewish culture and history in the twentieth century.

A vast, autonomous Jewish Yiddish culture developed in secular and religious communities in Europe and the Americas from the end of the nineteenth century until the Holocaust. More than 18,000 books in Yiddish were published in less than a hundred years. Scores of daily newspapers and magazines, theatres and schools, adult-education networks and libraries played an active role in the lives of the 5 million people who lived in a Yiddish cultural environment. Traces of this vibrant but short-lived flowering of Yiddish culture can be found in the works of Jewish creative artists in all fields and languages in the twentieth century.

The study of the present cultural life and creativity will include works illustrating the literature and rebirth of Hebrew as a spoken language in Eastern Europe and its influence in the creation of Israeli Hebrew secular culture beginning in the twentieth century; works representing Jewish reform movements and their contribution to the secularization process of Jewish populations and Diaspora culture in the Diaspora; and the works of messianic movements that encouraged the emergence of Jewish national secular movements, both Zionist and anti-Zionist. Works of plastic and performing arts that reflect the past and current cross influences of Jewish artists and Western cultures will also be studied.

SECULAR JUDAISM – THE CULTURE OF SECULAR JEWS

The study of secular Judaism, a culture that has been developing since the eighteenth century, is as important as the study of religious Judaism, which was the dominant characteristic of Jewish culture until the nineteenth century.

Secular Judaism presently constitutes the culture of the majority of the Jewish people. The literature, scholarship and art produced by non-religious Jews since the eighteenth century is the largest corpus of creative works existing in Judaism. A selection from this enormous body of works of Jewish secular literature and art will be presented in the study program as the common denominator of the various lifestyles of secular Jews – their beliefs and ideologies, the ways they relate to and celebrate their holidays, and their conceptions of themselves as Jews and as members of international civilization. The program will also make students aware of the problems and crises derived from the revolutionary secularization process.

The study of beliefs prevalent in secular Judaism will include those defined as atheism, agnosticism, pantheism and deism. Students will explore their characteristics and historical sources and background, as well as their differences and common denominators. Many members of religious Reform, Conservative and

Reconstructionist Jewish synagogue communities define their outlook as "secula," according to the 2001 surveys entitled *ARIS 2001* and *AJIS 2001* authored by Egon Mayer, Barry Kosmin and Ariella Keysar under the auspices of the Graduate Center of the City University of New York.

The study of the history of ideas in secular Judaism will include contemporary authors, philosophers and poets such as: Martin Buber, Gershon Sholem, Isaiah Berlin, Yosef Dan, Amos Oz, A.B. Yehoshua, Philip Roth, Yehuda Amichai, Saul Bellow, Chaim Cohen, Erich Fromm, Sidney Hook, Yehuda Bauer, Eliezer Shweid, Rachel Elior, Sherwin Wine, Woody Allen, Allan Dershowitz and Robert Pinsky. Some of the earliest secular works will also be included as a means of studying the development of a Jewish secular outlook: Spinoza, the European Jewish Enlightenment, Mendelssohn, the Jewish society for the scientific research of Jewish culture (founded in Germany at the beginning of the nineteenth century and including Heine, Zunz, Geiger, and Graetz), and the Jewish Enlightenment movement, which included Ranak (R. Nachman Krochmal), Micha, Smolenskin, Liberman, and Y.L. Gordon. Also included will be the Yiddish and Hebrew writers of the late nineteenth and early twentieth centuries – Mendele Mocher Sforim, Y.L. Peretz, Shalom Aleichem, Brenner, Bialik, Achad Ha'am, Berditchevsky and scores of others.

The Interdisciplinary study of Jewish secular culture will include the performing and plastic arts created by Jews over the past two hundred years in all media – music, theater, opera, painting, sculpture, architecture, cinematic arts and television. A selection of works in all these fields of Jewish creativity represents, in addition to the development of ideas, the rich culture of secular Jews everywhere, their links with other cultures and their reciprocal influences.

The study of secular Judaism as a culture will shed a new light on all past eras of Judaism. Within the secular culture of the nineteenth and twentieth centuries, a new scientific and critical approach to the sources and history of Judaism developed. A selection of the thousands of scientific research papers in this field will be the basis for the new study of Judaism as a culture.

Also included will be a study of the changes in celebrations and significance of the Jewish historical holidays, ceremonies and commemoration of life-cycle events. This major change in Jewish tradition marks, more than any other, the difference between the religious and secular Judaisms developing in Jewish culture at the present.

THE INFLUENCE OF SECULARIZATION ON JUDAISM

The program will explore the effect of the secularization process on trends and movements, on the development of a national consciousness and the Jewish state, and on Jewish education systems and their curricula. It will study the imprint of secularization in the West – on literature and philosophy from Shakespeare, Cervantes and Spinoza onwards. (This trinity heralded a world from which God, as a personal figure involving himself in human life, was totally absent.)

The program will also explore evidence of atheism in the ancient East (pre-Buddhist and early Buddhism), in Hellenistic and Roman writing (from the pre-Socratic philosophers to Lucretius), and in the diatribes of its medieval opponents. Magic will also be studied as a form of parascientific folk atheism proposing that man commands the skills and techniques to alter natural processes and forces at will, and that these skills do not have a divine source.

SUBJECT AREAS IN JUDAISM AS CULTURE STUDIES

- *The various definitions of key concepts in Judaism as culture:* Judaism, Jewishness, culture, civilization, humanism, pluralism, relativism and others.
- *Controversy and belief and in contemporary Judaism and its roots in the past:* Values versus commandments, democracy and religion, atheistic and religious interpretations of the Bible, conceptions of God.
- *Judaism as part of world civilization:* The effect of ancient and modern religions and cultures on the evolution of Judaism; the influence of Judaism on world civilization and culture.
- *Humanism and human rights in Judaism:* The Ten Commandments and the prophets' interpretation of the covenant; their opponents, past and present.

- *The encounter of Jewish ethnicities – multiculturalism in Judaism and Israel:* The cultural integration process, as opposed to autonomous cultural identity and enriched creativity.
- *Changes in Jewry's historical and cultural images:* Discoveries and critical re-evaluations, archaeological and historical research, novels, poetry and literary criticism.
- *The uniqueness of ethical monotheism in Judaism:* Its influence on the lives of Jews and other nations.
- *Zionism as differentiated from other nineteenth- and twentieth-century national liberation movements:* The revival of Hebrew and Hebrew culture in Palestine-Israel and its effect on all of Jewry's communities and traditions.

WHAT HAS CHANGED? THE STUDY OF JEWISH HERITAGE

The study of Jewish heritage from the point of view of *ma nishtana* ("what has changed?") is a new approach to studying tradition.

The starting point of each study unit, which centers on a festival or life-cycle ceremony practised in Jewish culture, will be the new contemporary forms and content introduced into it by the secularization process and the reform movements. The changes in the form, meaning and content of festivals and ceremonies over the three thousand years of Jewish culture characterize Judaism as a pluralistic and evolving culture.

The study units will answer the question, "What has changed and is still changing in popular customs, in the occasions marked for communal and family celebration, and in the entire body of tradition passed down to us from earlier generations?"

The topic will be explored on two levels:

(1) The experiential level: Students themselves will try out the process of creating new rites and ceremonies, by designing and composing new *Haggadahs* for Passover, for instance. To promote their creativity, students will read and review other works of art relating to the festivals and traditional customs.

(2) The theoretical level: Students will review and discuss issues and problems, as well as review studies and reports relating to ceremonial and festival practice. They will focus on how these practices evolved and how they relate to non-Jewish sources.

The following are examples of content areas for study units of the program "Jewish heritage – Festivals and Life Cycle Ceremonies:"

Yom Kippur

Why do relatively few Jews today observe the traditional prayers and fasting? How do the secular mark this festival? What forms have Yom Kippur festivals taken in the twentieth century?

How have customs, prayers and their meaning changed since the Second Temple era? Why in the Middle Ages did many religious and secular Jews object to the *Kol Nidrei* prayer, and why do many still object to it? What aspects of this prayer, releasing the petitioner from his oaths and vows, still convince many that it possesses exalted status?

What meaning does Yom Kippur have for freethinkers? How was it that Yom Kippur, in the Second Temple period, was a day for young men and women to perform courting dances (as described in the *Mishna*)?

What are the connections between the sacrifice of the scapegoat by the high priest in the Jerusalem Temple and similar customs in ancient Mesopotamia? Why do certain Orthodox groups persist in sacrificing animals on the eve of this holiday? Why were sacrifices offered in ancient times?

How did Maimonides, in *The Guide for the Perplexed* (Part 3, Chapter 32), explain the persistence of the practice of sacrifice, even after Jews had stopped "worshipping the foreign gods" (Maimonides' words) who required live sacrifice?

How did the Book of Jonah come to be associated with Yom Kippur, and what is its function in present-day Yom Kippur services, religious and secular? What role do works of art, literature and scholarship inspired by the Book of Jonah play in the secular observance of Yom Kippur? What is the nature of secular versions of Yom Kippur celebrations in secular humanistic synagogues in the US?

Passover – Rite and Ritual, Past and Present; The Seder *and the* Haggadah

A great variety of *Haggadahs* were created in the twentieth century for secular and religious communities. The study of a representative selection of new *Haggadahs* will introduce students to the various ways the holiday is celebrated in the present. The history of Passover, as documented in the Bible, the Talmudic literature and the "normative" *Haggadah* created in Iraq by the principals of the Sura religious college (Amram in the ninth century and Saadia in the tenth), will acquaint students with the history of Passover in the first two thousand years of its celebration.

The study of *Haggadahs* created during the Middle Ages and the Renaissance, and the paintings and poetry that were added to them, will be part of the study of the development of Jewish culture during these periods.

In modern times, extreme changes took place in the celebration and meaning of Passover. The study of a selection of literature devoted to Exodus, including its historical, ethical, religious and national aspects, will help secular students to create new *Haggadahs* and meaningful ways of celebrating Passover.

In non-Orthodox communities, modern *Haggadahs* and their accompanying ceremonies celebrate Passover as the holiday of spring, freedom and the creation of the Jewish nation. Erich Fromm and Michael Waltzer saw in the myth of Exodus the basis of humanism in Judaism. Instead of the *Haggadah* used by Amram and Saadiah a thousand years ago, which excluded Moses from its narrative and instead included texts from Midrashic literature, modern and secular *Haggadahs* include poems, readings and songs (traditional and new), as well as the biblical narrative of Moses and the Exodus story.

Students will grapple with questions such as the following:

- How is Passover celebrated in the modern era by various religious movements and ethnic communities, in secular homes and in communal celebrations?
- What is the unique contribution of the *Haggadahs* composed by the first Jewish secular communities in Jewish history – the kibbutzim of the twentieth century?
- In what terms does Michael Waltzer describe the effect of the Exodus saga on other peoples' cultures and liberation movements?

- How and why did the Passover festival develop from its origins as a family festival of sacrifice and feasting, where participants ate standing and dressed for a journey, into a national festival of pilgrimage and a central sacrifice ceremony in Jerusalem, until it reverted, under the influence of the Greek *symposium*, to being once more a home feast?
- Why did the *Haggadah* of Rabbis Amram and Saadiah eliminate the life and achievements of Moses from the Exodus saga? Why does this *Haggadah* take the bulk of its material from the *Midrash* (*Mekhilta*, *Sifrei*) rather than from the Bible, and how can this be explained by the schism between Rabbinic and Karaite Judaism?
- What are the arguments for restoring the biblical narrative and the story of Moses to a prime role in new *Haggadahs*?
- What contribution did the *Haggadah* make to the development of Jewish decorative and figurative arts during the Middle Ages and Renaissance?
- How can the statues and paintings, plays, operas and films on Exodus and Passover themes play a role in celebrations of Passover in the non-Orthodox Judaisms?

WOMEN'S STATUS IN JUDAISM

The study of women's status in Jewish culture and society will begin with the achievements and failures of the struggle for equality in the present. New legislation has instituted formal equality of women and men in most Jewish communities freed from religious *Halakhic* rules.

The traditional *Halakhic* legal system still deprives women of their right to full equality in the religious courts. These courts in Israel have legal status granted by the secular democratic state.

The study units will explore the sources and historical developments that contributed to the present status of women in Judaism. Questions to be considered include:

- Why is discrimination against women in the social, economic, political and moral spheres one of society's gravest problems?
- What measures and societal and educational reforms are needed to ensure that legal equality will become real equality between men and women?

- How and when did the status of women in Judaism start to change?
- How and why does the democratic Jewish state legitimate discriminatory laws and judicial rulings in matters of marriage and divorce?
- What light do literature and poetry, theater and cinema cast on women's status in Jewish civilization, past and present?
- To what extent is affirmative action justified and effective? What contribution might it have in achieving equal rights between men and women?
- What is the historical and sociocultural background of discrimination against women in Jewry and among other peoples?
- What do the Jewish sources say in support of and against discrimination and humiliation of women?
- How do the authors (male or female) of the books of the Bible show sympathy for central female characters who use sex to fight for their rights and status (e.g., Tamar, the wife of Er, and Ruth)?
- How does Genesis portray Eve as mutinying against an immoral divinity in order to provide humankind with knowledge and the capacity to tell good from evil?
- How has biblical exegesis distorted the conflict in Genesis by transferring responsibility for the "original sin" from God to Eve?
- What is the attitude of Moses (and the author of his story) to his marriage to a black wife and to those who oppose it? How do other biblical works treat marriages of Jewish men and non-Jewish women?
- How do the biblical authors relate to men's maltreatment of women such as Sarah, Hagar, Tamar (Amnon's sister) and Mikhal?
- What role do queens and goddesses play in the Bible, and what effect did they have on Jewish religious, cultural and social life?

THE VARIETY OF BELIEF IN RELIGIOUS JEWRY

The study program will explore the divergent beliefs, rites and conceptions of God in Jewry's religious movements, sects and ideologies – past and present:

- What are the prevalent beliefs of contemporary religious Jews (Reform, Conservative, Orthodox, and the various Kabbalistic and mystic sects)?
- What are the current influences of messianic medieval and Renaissance movements and beliefs?
- What were the dominant beliefs in the Hellenistic period of Judaism?
- What were the main beliefs of the Pharisees, Saducees, Essenes and Judeo-Christians – the authors of mystic literature?

THE BIBLE AS LITERATURE AND HISTORICAL DOCUMENTATION

The purpose of studying the stories and poems in biblical literature, which can and should be read as any great work of literature, is to introduce students to the classics of Judaism, the only corpus of writing considered the basis of all Judaisms in Jewish culture today.

Biblical stories and poetry will be treated as complete literary works to be appreciated by the reader aesthetically, emotionally and intellectually, though the editors of the Bible may have compiled them from many ancient sources.

The literary genres in the Bible are: the *novel* (such as the Genesis novel of matriarchs and patriarchs of the Jewish nation), the *historical novel* (such as the stories of Moses, Saul and David), the *short story* (Jonah, Ruth, Tamar, Esther and others), *religious poetry* in Psalms, *erotic secular poetry* in the Song of Songs, *philosophical drama and essay* (such as Ecclesiastes and Job), and the *poetic rhetoric* of the prophets.

The texts will be read in the *pshatt* tradition, that is, taking the plain meaning of the written word, as it is understood from other forms of usage in spoken and written Hebrew. Scientific analyses of contradictory, parallel versions of the same events and the multiple sources of texts will not be ignored. These will be studied as a separate syllabus unit on the history of the literary works of the Bible.

Reading the Bible as an anthology of superb examples of literary art is not a newly invented concept. The *magids* (wandering preachers) did so in their sermon-orations. Public readings of the biblical text, translated into the vernacular, followed the same idea. The intellectual and academic culmination of the concept came in the second half of the twentieth century with the Bible as Literature school, starting with Auerbachs's *Mimesis* and developed by leading authors and researchers such as Robert Alter, Frank Kermode, Harold Bloom, Shmaryahu Talmon, Meyer Sternberg, Ya'ir Zakowitz, Ya'ir Hoffman and Yaira Amit.

Reading the biblical text separately from later *Midrashic* creative exposition enhances the reader's emotional, aesthetic and intellectual experience with literary works that influenced many generations, making the Bible the most translated and most renowned literary text in the history of Western cultures and their spheres of influence. Many national cultures acknowledge Hebrew biblical works as part of their own "classic" literature (literary works that have retained the power to create an artistic experience and inspire and influence readers and artists throughout the generations).

Students of Jewish culture will acquaint themselves, through the reading of biblical literature, with the spiritual, religious and social attitudes prevalent in Jewish culture in the first thousand years of the formation of the Jewish people.

THE ARTS IN MODERN AND ANCIENT JUDAISM

The role that literature and other art forms played in Jewish culture will be studied *for each period* in the history of Judaism. The role of the arts in Judaism is neglected in most Jewish Studies programs. Painting and sculpture, theater, screenplays, poems, music and methods of performance have played a central role in the cultural life of the Jewish People since the days of the First Temple in Jerusalem. Orations and the art of rhetoric have had an important function in the development of Judaism since the era of the biblical prophets. The study of the arts in Judaism will enable students to understand the roles and aspects of Jewish culture expressed in these works.

The gallery of works in the plastic arts that played a role in ancient Jewish culture include statues of gryphons, Ashera, Baal and the Golden Calf, which represented Yahweh in the first temples in the desert and in Jerusalem, Beit El and Dan. Sculpted images were erected in the Second Temple in Jerusalem, and figurative mosaics and frescoes were found in synagogues of the Hellenistic period. Paintings adorned prayer books and Passover *Haggadahs* dating from the Middle Ages and Renaissance. According to the historians of Jewish art, Cecil Roth and Bezalel Narkiss, Jewish painting, manuscript illumination and book printing in the medieval and Renaissance periods represent continuity in the development of Jewish art. The hundreds of examples known to experts, and unknown to most students of Jewish culture, could change the general perception of Judaism.

The history of the performance arts also stretches back to the biblical and Hellenistic eras. Renaissance-period manuscripts from Central and Eastern Europe bear witness to the growth of a folk-theater tradition, of which a key component was the *purimspiel* – plays performed during the carnival and costume festival of Purim.

A few manuscripts in Hebrew (including the Italian Renaissance play of De Somi, *Tzahut Bdichuta Dekidushin*) and many manuscripts in Yiddish represent the presence of popular theatrical activity, which gave birth, in the nineteenth and twentieth centuries, to the professional theaters of Europe, the Americas and Israel.

The development of the arts of cinema and television created hundreds of films and programs that express Jewish problems and show how world culture plays an important role in the lives of Jews. These works can be an important source for studying particular aspects of Judaism. The study of film arts as part of the study of Judaism – including the many annual festivals in Europe, Israel and North America devoted to Jews in the cinema – help students to approach Judaism as a living and developing culture in all fields of human creativity.

HALAKHA AND LAW IN JUDAISM FROM A SECULAR POINT OF VIEW

An introduction to the study of this subject will describe the role and development of *Halakhic* religious laws in Jewish life today. The process leading to the non-observance of *Halakhic* laws by the majority of Jews is a central subject in the study of the changes in Judaism in the modern era. The various reforms and changes in *Halakhic* laws continue a tradition of change and development throughout the history of Jewish culture. This process of constant revision in Jewish religious laws becomes the main subject in the study of the Jewish religion. It includes an understanding of a relatively new phenomenon in Judaism – the minority Orthodox movement that started in the nineteenth century and tried unsuccessfully to arrest changes in the rules and laws governing Jewish life.

The collision between the system of democratically made state laws (which claim priority over *Halakhic*, Rabbinical law) and their opponents (who refuse to alter Rabbinical law) is one of the main issues in the war of cultures currently raging in Israel. Examples of Israel's Foundational Laws and the religious *Halakha* (including some religious laws recognized by the State of Israel) will illustrate the main controversies.

Students will trace the development of Jewish law and *Halakha* from the laws and commandments in Leviticus, Deuteronomy and other sections of the Bible, through the corpus of debate, dispute and majority decision in the Talmud, to *Responsa* literature, to various attempts to arrest the development of *Halakha* (Maimonides' *Mishne Torah*, Karo's *Shulkhan Arukh*), to the controversy over whether *Halakha* was a fixable code or a process. (By definition, the word *Halakha* derives from the Hebrew root *halakh*, meaning to walk, to proceed.)

The concept of the Oral Law, represented in the Jerusalem Talmud and the Babylonian Talmud, was a reform enterprise. The sages who participated in the discussion that changed biblical laws prohibited a written record of their deliberations and rulings in order to keep the process from becoming stagnant.

An examination of the religious laws in the Bible will reveal the many variants and contradictions among its rulings, proving that a process of change has characterized Judaism since the beginning of its religious development.

MESSIANISM FROM A SECULAR POINT OF VIEW

The phenomenon of Jewish messianism will be explored by analyzing the ideological and practical rivalry between secular Zionism (considered by many to be a kind of secular messianism, a movement that changed the course of Jewish history) and the religious messianic movements based on a Utopian vision of biblical prophets.

Jewish religious messianism in the eighteenth and nineteenth centuries, which held that Shabtai Tzvi was the actual messiah and next king of liberated Israel, played a role in the revival of Jewish national consciousness. According to Gershon Sholem, Sabbatean messianism aroused national aspirations and encouraged, after its failure, modern secular Zionism.

Jewish messianism, since the time of the biblical prophets, proposed the Utopia of redemption of the collective – the Israeli nation. Christian messianism, which developed within Judaism at a latter stage, proposed the redemption of the individual. Jewish religious messianism in modern times was systematic in its opposition to Zionism and the pragmatic programs that enabled the establishment of the State of Israel, since it opposed a return to the Jewish homeland before the coming of the Messiah.

The most important contribution of messianism to Jewish culture was the development of a faith in a better future, an ideal world, which became a driving force for new social and revolutionary movements in which Jews played major roles. The study of messianism in Judaism covers many areas and periods in Jewish history, from the biblical era to the present.

MYSTICISM FROM A SECULAR POINT OF VIEW

Mysticism in Jewish religious culture has yielded a wealth of philosophy, theology, magic, folklore, mythology and storytelling. Many secular scholars, among them Gershon Sholem and Yosef Dan, have studied and shed new light on this vast phenomenon and its evolution.

Students will discover how the terms "mysticism" and "rationalism" were defined at different stages of Jewish and world history, and how they have collided since the time of Maimonides and Nahmanides, at the beginning of the second millennium. They will also explore connections between the mysticism and magic practiced by various movements and sects. The study of the literature of mysticism and *Kabalah*, and of the practice of magic, are explicitly prohibited in the Bible. Nevertheless, such practices have been popular throughout Jewish history.

Among the works to be studied are the Book of Daniel; the literature of the *Merkava* (chariot), which carried its riders to encounters with angels in the divine Kings' celestial *Hekhalot* (palaces); and medieval writings such as the *Zohar*, the *Book of Hassidim*, the compositions of the Lurian school, tales of wonder-working Rabbis, and the legends of the *Golem of Prague*.

Specific topics will include:

- The development of *Kabbala* and the influence of the early mystical texts on groups of Jewish thinkers in medieval Provence, Spain and Safad.
- The spread of the *Kabbalah*'s influence on Jews through Hassidism, and the opposition to this trend.
- The centers of *Kabbalah* study and the practice of "practical *Kabbalah*" in modern times.
- Mysticism's creation of a Jewish mythology and the effect of the inventions of a next world and a life after death on the development of Judaism during the Hellenistic and medieval periods.
- The influence of *Kabbalah* and its mythology (that lesser divinities surround God and people our earthly world) on non-religious writing in the twentieth century.

THE INFLUENCE OF ATHEISTIC BELIEFS ON JUDAISM AND JEWRY

Objectives of the study program:

(1) To explore the rationalist-atheist belief system and assess its expanding role in Jewish culture and thinking.

(2) To evaluate the way religion is affected by scientific research on natural laws, and to assess technology's promise to improve the quality of human life.

Topics for study and discussion:

- The improved "quality of human life" as the goal of morality, science and technology.
- Elevating this goal into a principle governing social organization and political activity as powerful forces in the secularization of

all societies. (Jewish conceptions of Judaism changed when humanistic ideas replaced the belief that the goal of human activity was to serve the will of God and obey the commands religious leaders formulated in his name.)

- The comparative study of secularization processes in Western and Eastern cultures, including the history of atheist beliefs parallel to the history of religious beliefs.
- The influence of secularism and a variety of atheist beliefs – such as agnosticism, deism and pantheism – on the development of Jewish creativity and on Jewish education.
- The imprint of secularization on literature and philosophy, beginning in the seventeenth century, in masterpieces of modern Western culture. Spinoza, Shakespeare, Cervantes, for example, heralded a world from which God as a personal figure, involved in human life, was totally absent.
- Evidence of atheism in the ancient East (pre-Buddhist, Buddhist, Hellenistic and Roman writing – from the pre-Socratic philosophers to Lucrecius) and medieval underground spokesmen who described atheistic ideas in great detail in their seemingly critical attempt to refute them.

Historians of atheism considered magic theories and practices as forms of parascientific folk atheism, proposing that human beings command the skills and techniques to alter natural processes and forces according to their own will, and not that of a divinity. Atheism is to be studied in both its modes: (1) as a critical approach to religion and faith in the supernatural, and (2) as a positive set of beliefs in humanism and the human capacity to create systems of values and morality, to create gods and other cultural symbols of the laws of nature and human moral behaviour.

JUDAISM'S OPENNESS TO OTHER CULTURES: RECIPROCAL INFLUENCES

The study of reciprocal cultural relations between Judaism and other cultures enriches our knowledge of Jewish literary, religious and artistic creations, their affinity to other cultures, and of the peoples among whom Jews lived.

In contrast with other nomadic nations, Jews were always open to influences of neighboring cultures such as the Mesopotamian, Egyptian, Muslim, European Christian and, at present, American. Students will compare Jewish and non-Jewish cultures, assessing the extent of the influence of "foreign" cultures on Judaism and noting what has remained unique in Jewish culture. Examples of topics: the comparison between the two Genesis creation narratives and a much older Mesopotamian myth of creation (Enumaelish); comparisons of customs, rites, beliefs and written texts showing that Egyptian, Mesopotamian, Canaanite, Greek, Hellenistic, Hindu, Arab, Muslim, European Christian and secular Western sources were all represented in Jewish culture.

Since the first century, Jewish religion and culture have influenced the cultures of people on all continents through the Christian and Muslim religions. With the spread of Jews and Judaism across the Roman Empire, the development of Judeo-Christianity, and its departure from Rabbinical Judaism, fundamental elements of Judaism were carried into all parts of the world under Roman rule.

Ethical monotheism, the books of the Jewish Bible, the Sabbath and the synagogue are the most outstanding of Jewry's contributions to the world. Judaism's influence is most prevalent in the Christian and Islamic worlds, albeit with significant alterations. Its texts continue to exert their influence, even in the secular humanist society of the modern West. Many of the books of the Jewish Bible are now the classics of non-Jewish peoples and cultures, and their translations into local vernaculars have changed even the language and literature of these cultures.

The revolutionary and unprecedented social concept of the Sabbath organized the passage of time according to human needs rather than divine nature. Six days of work were now followed by a seventh of leisure, decreed in egalitarian statutes, which granted the right and obligation of rest to everyone, including domesticated animals. In its manifold adaptations, the Sabbath is now a universal institution.

The synagogue is a revolutionary innovation in the history of religion and culture. The antithesis of the temple, the synagogue represents a major turning point in the history of organized religion. The temple, the House of God, gave way to a house of the human community; a center of sacrificial rite gave way to a place where the community assembled for cultural, educational activity and prayer. A community based on tribe and clan gave way to a community of culture. This radical new social idea was also adopted by Christianity and Islam throughout the world.

The destruction of the Temple in Jerusalem decentralized and dispersed Judaism's priestly establishment. The synagogue was an autonomous institution, self-sustaining and independent of any hierarchy of priests and rabbis. This autonomous status enabled Jews to maintain their religious and national identity while choosing the kind of Judaism they wanted to adopt. The variety and mobility enhanced pluralism in Judaism.

The fragmentation of liturgy, rite and traditional practice was enhanced by the establishment of local synagogues in the widening Diaspora. The synagogue is a community, cultural and religious center. Historically, it served a variety of needs – a learning center for children and adults, a community court of justice, a site for interest-free banking, help for the sick and a place to receive guests.

The temple was led and managed by hereditary-based casts, or by kings who became priests. The synagogue is directed by members of the community who appoint or dismiss their rabbis. People could establish or join new synagogues because of ideological or religious beliefs, or leave at will and transfer to other communities.

New movements and synagogues grew rapidly. In less than a hundred years (in the eighteenth and nineteenth centuries) Chasidism became one of the major Orthodox religious movements in Judaism. The Reform, Conservative and Reconstructionist movements and synagogues became the majority of religious Judaism in the twentieth century.

Revolutionary changes have taken place in the synagogue in the modern period: the majority of religious Jewry rejects special sections for women in synagogues and has ended the ban on women's eligibility for the Rabbinate and communal leadership.

In the second half of the twentieth century, secular synagogues were founded in the US and Canada. They retained the communal and cultural aspects of synagogues, without their religious characteristics. Services are conducted as secular celebrations of the Sabbath, holidays and life-cycle events of the members of the community.

GLOSSARY

Afikoman The name of Greek origin given to the middle of the three leaves of *matzo* (unleavened bread) put on the ceremonial Passover plate at the beginning of the *seder*. A popular custom is for the *seder* leader to hide half of it at the beginning of the evening and for the children present to search for it at some later stage. The finder is usually promised a present.

Ahab King of Israel, c. 874–852 BCE. Very successful in military and foreign affairs but harshly condemned by the prophets for his tyrannous treatment of the small farmer and for allowing the establishment of the cults of Baal and Ashtoreth. Ahab, say the books of Kings, built a sanctuary to Baal in the very center of his city, Samaria, and 450 priests of Baal and 400 prophets of Asherah ate at his Queen Jezebel's table.

Ahad Ha'am The pen name (it means "one of the people") taken by Asher Hirsch Ginsberg, 1856–1927, Hebrew essayist and polemicist, and one of the most influential thinkers of his generation. His influence was especially great on the development of secular Judaism.

Akhenaton Egyptian pharaoh who reigned c. 1367–1350 BCE. Akhenaton has been credited with introducing monotheism even before Moses by making Aton the paramount deity of Egypt. Belief in Aton died with the death of Akhenaton.

Alter, Robert Professor of Hebrew and Comparative Literature at the University of California at Berkeley. Literary critic and biblical translator. One of the leaders of the Bible as Literature school of biblical interpretation.

Alterman, Nathan (1910–70). One of the most famous Israeli poets, renowned for his brilliant imagery and wit.

Amram (d. c. 875) Gaon (president) of the great Torah academy of Sura in Babylonia. His fame rests primarily on his *Seder* (more commonly *siddur*) "the order of prayers and blessings for the entire year" and the oldest extant ordering of Jewish prayers, including the Passover *Haggadah.*

Apocrypha A group of books of Jewish literature, mainly of the Second Temple period, excluded from the biblical canon but allowed into the canon of the Roman Catholic and Greek Orthodox bibles. The Talmud (see below) termed them *Sefarim Khitzonim* ("extraneous books") and, apart from the Wisdom of Ben Sira, there is not a single reference to them in the whole of Talmudic literature. Other famous references are Tobit and the four Books of the Maccabees (R. Akiba threatened all who read the latter with "loss of their place in the world to come'").

Asherah Canaanite fertility and mother goddess, apparently the consort of El, father and creator of the gods. The Asherah cult was widespread in both Jewish kingdoms, Israel and Judah.

Ashtoreth Sister and consort of Baal, she is the pre-eminent pagan goddess in the Bible. She is both a warrior goddess and goddess of sexual love and fertility. Popular in both kingdoms, Ashtoreth's cult was promoted by King Solomon. King Josiah later destroyed the cult palaces Solomon had built for her.

Baal The great weather god of the Western Semites, guarantor of the rains on which all inhabitants of the region depend. The allure of Baal-worship, featuring sexual practices, captivated the Israelites even before they reached Canaan, and his cult persisted throughout the following centuries in both kingdoms, as the tirades of the prophets tell us.

Bar-mitzvah, Bat-mitzvah A boy or girl who has reached the age of responsibility, the boy at 13, the girl at 12. Those who are religious are from that age traditionally obliged to fulfil all the religious commandments. The ceremony marking this occasion is often celebrated by secular Jews as a festive rite of passage. The popularity of *bat-mitzvah* ceremonies is much more recent than the ancient *bar-mitzvah* ritual.

Bialik, Haim Nahman (1873–1934): Poet, essayist, and story-writer in Hebrew, translator and editor, he has exercised an enormous influence on modern Jewish and Israeli secular culture. His 1913 essay, *On the Hebrew Book*, propounds the idea of selecting, assembling and publishing the best of classic Jewish writing of all periods.

Bloom, Harold Sterling Professor of Humanities at Yale University, Berg Professor of English at New York University, and renowned literary critic and scholar. One of the leading scholars of the Bible as Literature school of biblical interpretation.

Buber, Martin (1878–1965): Jewish philosopher and theologian, Zionist thinker and leader. He sees human relationships as I–Thou (a true dialogue, both partners speak to one another as equals) or I–It (not a true dialogue, in which one uses the other to achieve some end). Men and women know God, the Eternal Thou, through particular I–Thou relationships with persons, animals, nature and works of art, not through cognitive propositions. Revelation is never a formulation of law.

Caro, Joseph (1488–1575): Rabbi, mystic, Talmudic scholar and author of the *Shulkhan Arukh* (see below), a comprehensive codification of Jewish law (*Halakha*).

Cave of the Machpelah According to the Bible, Abraham bought the cave from Ephron the Hittite as a burial place for his wife, Sarah. Abraham himself, Isaac and Rebecca, Jacob and Leah are all buried there. The location of the cave is thought to be within the Haram El-Khalil mosque in Hebron, itself the reconstruction of a Byzantine church, but remains on the site go back to at least the first century CE. There is currently a mosque and a synagogue on the site.

Cohen, Hermann (1842–1918): German Jewish philosopher and interpreter of Kant. Defended Judaism against anti-Semitic attacks. He interpreted *mitzva* (see below) to mean both law and duty and believed that the law originates in God, the sense of duty in man. Cohen rejected Zionism, seeing in it a betrayal of the messianic ideal of the unity of humankind.

Conservative Judaism A movement that developed in Europe and the US. Conservative Jews welcomed emancipation, the end of ghettoization, the separation of church and state, and the Westernization of manner, education and culture. They affirmed that changes in Judaism could be made validly in the light of biblical and rabbinic precedent. They retained as essential a Hebrew liturgy, *kashrut* and the Sabbath.

Derash A method of interpreting the biblical text that allows, even encourages, the reader to find in the words, and even in individual letters, hidden meanings or meanings "alluded to." It is extensively used in preparing *midrash,* i.e., elaborations on a text for the purpose of teaching a religious or moral lesson. The opposite method is *pshatt.*

Dura Europos A city of ancient Babylon on the River Euphrates. Its third-century-CE synagogue was discovered in 1932 in a remarkable state of preservation. The interior walls are covered with frescoes of biblical scenes and personages. Its two most significant aspects are that (a) the Jews of the time did not hesitate to decorate a synagogue with the human form, and (b) the artists' fusion of Jewish, Hellenistic and Persian elements predates by centuries the same fusion that formed the basis of Byzantine Christian art.

Edomites The people of Edom, the Land of Israel's southeastern neighbor. According to the Bible, Edom is the land of Esau, Jacob's brother. Hasmonean King John Hyrcanus forcibly converted all the Edomites to Judaism. Hyrcanus's successor, Alexander Yannai, made the Edomite Antipas ruler of Edom, and his grandson, Herod, was appointed king of Judea by the Romans.

Elijah Israelite prophet and miracle-worker. Active in the Kingdom of Israel in the reign of Ahab (ninth century BCE), Elijah battled for Yahwist monotheism against the polytheist *Baal* worship. He defeated the Baalist prophets in a contest of miracle-making, which led to their massacre.

Elohim Gods. Also one of the many names of Israel's God, as borrowed from the Canaanites. The many other names for *Elohim* include *Yahweh, El Shaddai, Adonai, El Olam* and *El Ro'i.*

Essenes A Jewish ascetic sect and communal brotherhood of the Second Temple period, active from the second century BCE to the end of the first century CE. The Essenes withdrew from the "inadequate" ritual purity of the Temple establishment in Jerusalem to a nearly monastic commune on the shore of the Dead Sea. They are identified by some scholars as the authors of the Dead Sea Scrolls.

Frankists Followers of Jacob Frank (1726–91), a pseudo-messiah, whose sect constituted the last stage in the development of the Sabbatean movement. Frankism combined sexual license with a non-Orthodox interpretation of Torah. Frank and his sect later converted to Christianity.

Fromm, Erich (1900–80): American Jewish psychoanalyst, social philosopher and author. He postulated two major kinds of religion, authoritarian and humanistic. He believed in the latter, in which man experiences oneness with the "all" and achieves his greatest strength and self-realization.

Gaon (plural: Gaonim) The formal title of the heads of the great Torah academies of Sura and Pumbedita in Babylonia (modern-day Iraq). From the seventh to the eleventh centuries CE, the Gaonim were recognized by many Jews as the supreme doctrinal authority (see *Amram, Saadiah*).

Gemara A word popularly applied to the Talmud as a whole, the discussions and elaborations on the *Mishna* made by scholars in the third, fourth and fifth centuries CE who created the Oral Law.

Golem of Prague A *golem* is a monstrous creature, created by magic and the use of the holy name. Based on belief that the letters of the name of God and the Torah possess the power to create, this legend tells of Rabbi Judah Loew of Prague and the ancient Prague synagogue, the Altneuschul. Rabbi Judah created a *golem*-servant but turned him to dust when he ran amok. Many twentieth-century writers, artists and musicians were inspired by the legend.

Guide for the Perplexed Maimonides is the greatest Jewish philosopher of the Middle Ages and his *Guide*, composed in Arabic around 1200 CE, is acknowledged to be the most important philosophic work by a Jew of that period. Maimonides understood the anthropomorphic terms the Bible uses in relation to God as having an allegorical and spiritual meaning and not as an actual description of the Divine Being.

Habiru A social grouping of nomads in the Fertile Crescent of the Middle East during the second millennium BCE (beginning in the eighteenth century BCE). Although they were Western Semites, Habiru are often identified with the biblical term *ivri* (Hebrew) and are a point of historical and philological controversy.

Haggadah A set form of blessings, prayers, Midrashic comments and psalms fixing the order of activities (*seder*) for the ritual Passover meal. The most famous *Haggadah*, used throughout the religious Jewish world, was composed by Rabbis Amram and Saadiah, leaders of the Babylonian Jewish community in the ninth and tenth centuries CE. The twentieth century witnessed the composition of numerous modern *Haggadahs*, both religious and secular.

Halakha (plural: Halakhot) A code of rules and commandments (and associated discussions) covering all personal, social, national and international relationships and all religious practices and observances of Judaism. *Halakha* can refer to the whole corpus of law or to one particular law or ruling. The *Halakha* accumulated and developed over time, as scholars interpreted the Written Law (Torah), creating many new rulings in the framework of the Oral Law (the Talmuds), which are still being made today.

Halevi, Yehuda (c.1075–1141) Hebrew poet and philosopher. About 800 poems of his are known, including religious and secular works, love poems, songs of Zion, eulogies for famous figures, and *piyyutim*. His works, which voice personal religious experiences, are considered great achievements of the Hebrew language. It was rare at the time to believe, as Halevi did, that the Jews could attain their ideal existence only in the Land of Israel. He died on his journey to settle there.

Haskalah The Jewish Enlightenment movement and ideology, which began in the 1770s. Rooted in the general European Enlightenment of the eighteenth century (influenced by Spinoza), it responded to specifically Jewish problems. It was a movement that drew, for the most part, those who held (as Maimonides had) that secular studies should be a legitimate element of a Jewish education.

Hasmoneans The priestly family that headed the rebellion of the Judean Jews (started 168 BCE) against the Seleucid rulers, who were trying to suppress their Jewish religion. The Seleucids were driven out (the victory celebrated by the Hanukkah festival), and the Hasmoneans re-established a sovereign Jewish kingdom and a ruling dynasty. Both flourished for about a hundred years, until the area of Palestine was annexed by the Romans.

Hassidism A popular religious movement and form of communal organization that emerged in Eastern European Jewry in the late eighteenth century. It was characterized by mass enthusiasm to the point of ecstasy and the tight-knit cohesion of communities around a charismatic *rebbe* (rabbi), called *zadic* (the righteous). The movement won acknowledgment as a legitimate Jewish phenomenon and remains a strong element in Orthodox Jewry today (see *Khabad*).

Heine, Henrich (1797–1856): German Jewish poet (one of the greatest ever lyric poets of the German language) and essayist. Heine was baptized a Lutheran in 1825 solely in order to earn a doctorate and a career (in vain), and he retained an ambiguous attitude to this act all his life. Many consider him one of the first secular Jewish writers.

Hekhalot The *Hekhalot* literature of the early centuries CE is extremely important in the development of Jewish mysticism.

Hekhalot means "palaces" and refers to the heavenly palaces of God, to which famous initiates such as Rabbis Akiva and Ishmael ascended in a chariot (*merkava*). (See *Merkava* and *Shiur Qomah*.)

Hellenizers The name used to designate those Jews who were influenced by Hellenstic culture (from third century BCE to the fifth century CE). Hellenizing Judaism – a vast phenomenon comprising many flourishing communities in the Diaspora and the Land of Israel – created a rich corpus of literary and artistic works. It was bitterly resisted and fought by the rabbinic (Pharisee) sector of Jewry in the Land of Israel, reaching the point of civil war against the Hellenizing Hasmonean court.

Herod, King of Judea (ruled 37–4 BCE): Edomite by ancestry (the Edomites had been forcibly converted to Judaism) and put on the throne of Judea by Romans, Herod was both supported and hated by Jews. He ruled mercilessly and efficiently and was a builder of magnificent towns, palaces, temples and fortresses. The incomparable culmination of this fervor was his rebuilding and enlarging of the Jerusalem Temple.

Hillel the Elder The greatest of the sages of the Second Temple period and *Nasi* (president) of the Jewish supreme court of law. The height of his influence was from 10 BCE to 10 CE. He brought about a revolution in Israel's spiritual-intellectual life and founded a judicial dynasty that ruled Jewish life for over 400 years.

Jason of Cyrenaica Mid-second-century-BCE Jewish historian, who wrote a five-volume history of the Maccabean revolt. Though the work has been lost, a summary forms part of the Second Book of the Maccabees.

Jeremiah One of the major prophets who espoused the principle that social justice has priority over ritual and sacrifice. Active from 627 BCE to the Babylonian conquest and exile of Judea in 587 BCE, Jeremiah saw the Babylonians and their ruler, Nebuchadnezzar, as the instrument of God's punishment of Judea for abandoning the moral principles of the Covenant. He therefore preached submission to Nebuchadnezzar as the will of God. King Zedekiah refused,

Jerusalem fell, and the elite were exiled. (See *Nebuchadnezzar, Zedekiah.*)

Josephus (38 CE–c. 100 CE): Jewish historian, the most important historical source for the reign of Herod and the great revolt against Rome (66–73 CE). A prodigy of Torah learning in his youth who wrote in Greek and admired Roman culture, Josephus commanded Galilee against the Romans in the revolt and surrendered. He was granted Roman citizenship and a pension, settled in Rome under Imperial favor, and there wrote his history of the revolt, *The Jewish War*, and the history of the Jewish People. He was also the first Jewish scholar to conduct polemics against anti-semitism.

Judeo-Christians A Jewish sect whose leaders were Jesus of Nazareth and the authors of the Jewish writings known as the New Testament. Their belief in Jesus as Messiah eventually separated their development of Judaism from the traditional Judaism of the time and became the foundation for Christianity.

Kabbalah The mystical stream in Judaism, expressing the desire for immediate awareness of, and communion with, God. In the twelfth and thirteenth centuries CE, the *Kabbalah* was influenced by early Jewish mystical texts (*Hekhalot* and *Merkava* literature, see above and below), gnosticism and neo-Platonism. Its most famous expression is the *Zohar* of thirteenth-century Spain. The *Kabbalah* achieved a much more popular status in the sixteenth century under the influence of Lurian *Kabbalah* (see below) from Safad (see also *Sabbateanism*) and in the eighteenth century with the rise of Hassidism (see above). Theoretical and practical *Kabbalah* differ in that the latter uses magical formulae to alter reality (bring luck, heal illness, create a golem etc.). Central to theoretical *Kabbalah* is the doctrine of the *Sefirot*, 10 divine potencies (*sefirot* emanating from *einsof*, infinitude). *Tikkun* – a complete "restoration" leading to redemption and the advent of the Messiah – is believed to come about through meditation, *mitzva* observance, and Torah study.

Karaites A Jewish mass movement of the eighth century CE. The Karaites recognized only the Five Books of Moses as the source of Jewish religious law and, like the Sadducees, rejected the authority of all later *Halakhic* development of the Oral Law, Mishna, Talmud etc. Once quite large in number, there are only a few thousand Karaites today.

Kermode, Frank Literary critic and biblical scholar of the Bible as Literature school of interpretation.

Khabad (the Lubavicher Hassidim) A movement founded by Shneur Zalman of Lyady in Belorussia, within the wider Hassidic branch of Judaism, in the late eighteenth century. Khabad stresses intellectuality, hence its name, an acronym of ***Kh**okhma* (wisdom), ***B**inah* (understanding), ***D**a'at* (knowledge). Today, it is perhaps the most actively outgoing of all Hassidic sects in its drive to bring Jews back to Orthodoxy. It has recently incurred the wrath of other sectors of Orthodoxy for all but proclaiming its last rabbi as the King-Messiah, a deed considered to be just short of idolatry (see *Hassidism, Vilna Gaon*).

Kheruv (plural: kheruvim) A winged, celestial, gryphon-like being mentioned in the Bible in several contexts. Two carved images of *kheruvim* flanked the Ark in the Tabernacle. Two huge *kheruvim* statues guarded the Ark in the Holy of Holies in Solomon's Temple, their wings stretching from wall to wall.

Kibbutz (plural: kibbutzim) Communal farming and industrial settlements, which, from the establishment of the first kibbutz (Degania) in 1909, were based on principles of common property and wealth. All members worked for the collective, which assumed responsibility for all needs. Today, there are some 240 kibbutzim, which account for 2–3 per cent of the total population of Israel. Many elements of the communal way of life are in process of "privatization."

Korakh The central figure in the biblical episode recounting a revolt against the authority and status of Moses and Aaron during the wanderings in the wilderness (see Numbers 16).

Lilith A female demon, central to Jewish demonology from the time of antiquity. Kabbalist mythology makes her the permanent partner of Samael, king of the realm of evil, and thus parallel in function to the *Shekhina* (Divine Presence), mother of the House of Israel (see below).

Lurian Kabbalah Isaac Luria (known as *Ha-Ari*, 1534–72), was the pre-eminent Kabbalist of his age and a powerful influence on the subsequent development of *Kabbalah*. He lived in Safad, Northern Israel, and his teachings were written down by his disciple, Haim Vitale.

Maccabees "The Maccabee" was the name given to Judah, son of Mattathias the Hasmonean, who led the Jewish revolt against the Seleucids to its first crucial victories. He purged the temple of pagan ritual and founded the Hanukkah festival, but died in battle before Judea's independence was finally established by his younger brothers. The name came to be applied to the family as a whole and to the Hasmonean royal dynasty (see Hasmoneans).

Maggid A popular and usually itinerant preacher. The maggids were a strong tradition in Europe beginning in the late Middle Ages, and some historians have ascribed to them the role of a non-establishment intelligentsia, having much of the learning and influence of the established scholars, but unshackled by the ensconced rabbis' connections to the upper strata of Jewish society.

Mendele Mokher Seforim (1835–1917): The pen-name (meaning Mendele the Bookseller) of Shalom Abramowitz, Hebrew and Yiddish essayist, novelist and short-story writer in Russia. One of the founders of modern literary Yiddish and the new realism in Hebrew literature.

Mendelssohn, Felix Bartholdy (1809–47): A composer with successful parents (his father was a banker) who had all their children baptized. The children later voluntarily converted to Christianity. Felix refused his father's pressure to drop their Jewish-sounding surname in favor of Bartholdy alone.

Merkavah *Merkavah* means "chariot," and *Merkavah* literature is a branch of early Jewish mysticism (first centuries CE), which aspired to the vision of the Divine Throne on its Chariot (see Ezekiel 1) and to contemplate the mysteries of the Divine Glory. (See *Hekhalot*.)

Metatron An angel accorded special distinction in Jewish esoteric and mystical doctrine beginning in the first century CE. He is often ascribed a power exceeding that of all similar divine beings and less only than that of Yahweh himself.

Midrash (plural: Midrashim) A genre of rabbinical literature. A *midrash* is the extended creative exegesis of a biblical text, which formed the basis for the development of legends and points of *Halakha*.

Mishna *Mishna* is the Hebrew name for the first collection of the Oral Law. The *Mishna* refers to the six orders (sections) of the Oral Law redacted, arranged and revised at the beginning of the third century CE by Yehuda Ha-Nasi, the venerated rabbi-ruler of Judean Jewry.

Mishne Torah Maimonides' great classification by subject matter of the *Halakha* of all Talmudic and post-Talmudic literature in 14 volumes, the first such systematic codification. His achievement awed the scholarly world but generated huge controversy.

Mitnagdim The *Mitnagdim* ("opponents") are a movement opposed to Hassidism. (See *Hassidism* and *Vilna Gaon*.)

Mitzva A commandment or religious *Halakha*. Traditionally, there are 613 biblical commandments, 248 of them positive and 365 prohibitive. They were followed by an additional category of rabbinical commandments.

Moloch An apparently Assyrian deity, whose cult was introduced by King Ahaz of Judah (743–727 BCE) and was firmly established in Jerusalem in the reigns of Manasseh and his son Amon. In the final years of the First Temple period, Jeremiah denounced the cult for its practice of child sacrifice.

Nakhmanides, Rabbi Moses Ben Nakhman (RaMBaN) (1194–1270): One of the leading Talmudists of Middle Age Spanish Jewry. A philosopher, Kabbalist, biblical commentator, poet and physician.

Narkiss, Bezalel Leading historian of Jewish art and professor at Hebrew University, Jerusalem.

Nebuchadnezzar Ruler of Babylon, 605–562 BCE. First invaded Palestine in 604 BCE, forcing all its kings, among them Yehoiakhin of Judah, to pay tribute. A few years later, some of the kings rebelled, and in 597 BCE, Nebuchadnezzar invaded again, this time capturing Jerusalem and Yehoiakhin, and choosing his own king for Judah – Zedekiah. In 589 BCE, Zedekiah rebelled. In the following year Jerusalem was besieged, and in 586 BCE, it was burned and destroyed. A large part of the Judean population was exiled to Babylonia.

Oral Law The Oral Law is the authoritative Talmudic interpretation of the Written Law (the Torah). Many sectors of Jewry have opposed this authority, among them the Sadducees, the Karaites, and certain modern movements in Judaism.

Orthodoxy Orthodox Judaism considers itself the authentic bearer of the ancient religious Jewish tradition. As a well-defined movement within Judaism, it took shape in reaction to the challenge of the Haskalah, Reform Judaism and trends towards secularization in Western and Central Europe in the first half of the nineteenth century. The term "Orthodoxy," unknown in Judaism before 1795, has come to designate Jews who maintain the divine inspiration of the whole historical religion as recorded in the Written and Oral Law, and who observe it as codified in the *Shulkhan Arukh*. Today the term refers to the Orthodox minority within the religious sector of world Jewry.

Pharisees A sect of Judaism that came to be a political force after the successful Hasmonean revolt (168–160 BCE). Its followers developed and taught the Oral Law. By the first century CE they had come to represent the traditional attitudes and interests of the Jewish priestly caste in opposition to the Sadducees domination of the Temple and the religious establishment (see *Sadducees*). Unlike the Sadducees, the Pharisees believed in life after death.

Philo of Alexandria (c. 20 BCE–50 CE): Jewish philosopher and historian and one of the spokesmen of Alexandrian Jewry. He wrote in a high-level Greek (he probably knew no Hebrew), which, together with his knowledge of classical literature, philosophy, rhetoric and general science, he probably obtained in Greek schools. Philo read the Bible in its Septuagint translation into Greek. Rabbinical Judaism "excommunicated" his writings. He had a much greater philosophical influence on Christian thinkers than on Jewish thinkers, though in modern times his work is considered an important part of Jewish culture.

Piyyut Hebrew liturgical poetry, lyrical compositions incorporated into the obligatory prayer service or other religious ceremonies. The earliest known examples date from the first centuries CE. The golden age of *piyyut* was at the time of Spanish Jewry of the tenth to the twelfth centuries CE, the outstanding *paytanim* being Solomon ibn Gabirol, Moses ibn Ezra, Yehuda Halevi and Abraham ibn Ezra.

Pshatt The literal, unelaborated reading of a biblical text. It interprets words and sentences in the Bible according to their multiple uses in the Hebrew language. The opposite approach is *derash* (see above).

Purimspiel In the fourteenth and fifteenth centuries, an amateur monologue or group performance given at the traditional Purim meal in private homes. The subject matter was mainly humorous (frequently profane and/or obscene), partly traditional (from the Book of Esther and other biblical stories), and partly drawn from contemporary Jewish life. By the eighteenth century, the Purimspiel developed into publicly performed complex dramas with several thousand rhymed lines, large casts and musical accompaniment.

Reconstructionist Judaism An ideology and movement in modern US Jewry, owing its inspiration to Mordechai Kaplan. Kaplan argued that Judaism must transform itself from a civilization oriented in the hereafter into one that helps Jews attain salvation in this world. Salvation, in his view, is the progressive improvement of the human personality and the establishment of a free, just and cooperative social order.

Reform Judaism Also known as Liberal or Progressive Judaism, it was the first of the nineteenth-century responses to the situation of European Jews after Emancipation (see *Conservative Judaism*). Reform Judaism's many variants all assert the legitimacy of change and the denial of eternal validity to any given formulation or codification of Jewish law. Beyond that, Reform Jews display little unanimity of belief or observance. Conservative and radical positions coexist and enjoy mutual respect. This is the largest denomination in religious Jewry today.

Responsa The written responses of *Halakhic* authorities to those consulting them on problematic issues. Known from the early centuries CE, the *responsa* literature accumulated over time into a vast corpus of literary and historical importance. It is a prime source, for instance, for the history of Jewish communities worldwide. *Responsa* are still requested today in both Orthodox and Reform Judaisms.

Roth, Cecil (1899–1970): British Jewish historian of Jewish civilization and editor-in-chief of the *Encyclopaedia Judaica*. He also studied and collected Jewish art and conducted the first modern scientific study of illuminated Passover *Haggadahs*.

Saadiah (882–942): Gaon (president) of the Torah academy of Sura in Babylonia, philosopher and leader of Babylonian Jewry. Saadia made outstanding contributions to Hebrew philology and grammar and was an expert mathematician and astronomer. He produced the first Arabic translation of the Bible.

Sabbateanism The mass messianic ferment named after the "messiah," Shabtai Zvi (1626–76), the largest messianic movement in Jewry since the Bar Kokhba Revolt in the second century CE. All sectors of European and North African Jewry, Ashkenazi and

Sephardi, were influenced by it. Public demonstrations of rejoicing and mass hysteria were common. When the news came, in August 1666, of the Messiah's conversion to Islam under pressure from the Turkish authorities who had arrested him, many followers continued to believe in him and remained committed to the movement. (See *Frankists*.)

Sadducees A Jewish sect formed about 200 BCE, composed largely of the wealthy elements of society (priests, merchants, landowners). The sect dominated the temple worship and administration and was a strong force in political and economic policy. Its followers believed in the exclusive authority of the Torah (the Written Law) and rejected the idea of life after death. They refused to accept any ruling based on the Oral Law, which was the province of Pharisee rabbis (see *Pharisees*).

Samaritans The Northern Israelites who remained in the Land of Israel after the Assyrians exiled the elite of the Northern Kingdom in 722 BCE. When, in 538 BCE, the exiled Jews in Babylonia returned to Jerusalem, hostility developed between the two groups. The Samaritans tried to prevent the rebuilding of Jerusalem's walls. In 128 BCE, the Hasmonean king, John Hyrcanus, demolished the Samaritan's Temple on Mount Gerizim (Nablus). Samaritan Judaism accepts only the authority of the Pentateuch. Today, a few hundred remain in Israel.

Secular Jews Secular Jews are Jews who regard themselves as part of the authentic succession of Judaism and full heirs to its civilization, culture and history. They believe that Judaism is a culture that, like all cultures, includes religion. They do not accept the *Halakhic* code as the binding authority in their lives, and they hold various views about the existence and meaning of "God." Many believe "God" has no reality or role beyond that devised by human beings.

Seder *Seder* means "order" and refers to the customary order of prayer, ritual, feasting and other activities on holy days. The most famous *seder* is that of the first evening of the Passover festival, which is written in the Passover *Haggadah* (see *Haggadah*).

Septuagint The first translation of the Pentateuch into Greek, produced in Alexandria, Egypt, during the first half of the third century BCE. The name was then extended to the rest of the Bible and the non-canonical books as they were translated into Greek over the next two centuries. *Septuaginta* is "seventy" in Latin, relating to the legend that 72 elders of Israel, six from each tribe, were invited to Alexandria to carry out the translation.

Shammai (c. 50 BCE–c. 30 CE): Hillel the Elder's colleague as president of Judaism's supreme court of law. Like Hillel, he founded a great dynasty and school of law-makers, *Bet Shammai* (House of Shammai), which tended to rule more stringently than the school of Hillel.

Shekhina The Divine Presence. When God sanctifies a place, object or individual, the *Shekhina* is said to rest there. In medieval *Kabbalah* (see above), *Shekhina* represents the feminine entity whose union with the masculine God was broken by Israel's exile. Because of her femininity and closeness to the created world, she is the first target of satanic power and it is therefore the duty of humankind to protect her. In certain Kabbalist myths, she is presented as a female divinity.

Shiur Qomah *Shiur qomah* means "measure of the body." The book of *Shiur Qomah* is a genuine but highly enigmatic part of early Jewish mysticism (first and second centuries CE), which contemplates the fantastically huge dimensions of the divine body and limbs.

Shtetl The Yiddish word for the entirely or mainly Jewish small towns/large villages in which most of Eastern Europe's Jews lived between the sixteenth and nineteenth centuries. The fixed points of *shtetl* life were synagogue, home and market. A unique sociocultural pattern developed, dissolving in the nineteenth century when persecution, economic depression, political revolutions and the attractions of the modern world and secularization triggered mass emigration from the country to the cities of Europe and the Americas.

Shulkhan Arukh Joseph Caro's codification of Jewish law. First printed in 1565, it was amended by Moses Isserles and accepted as authoritative by all religious Jews. Orthodox Jewry continues to accept it as such. (See *Caro*.)

Sofer, Hatam (1762–1839): *Halakhic* scholar and leader in Orthodoxy. Sofer led Orthodoxy's struggle against the Reform and Haskalah movements, deliberately creating an irreparable breach between the Orthodox and non-Orthodox sectors of Jewry. His most famous (notorious) saying is *"Hadash asur min haTorah,"* i.e., even the slightest innovation is forbidden by the Torah.

Spinoza, Baruch (1632–77): Jewish philosopher and one of the fathers of secularism. He was excommunicated for heresy by the Portuguese Jewish community of Amsterdam, where he lived, after questioning (among other things) whether Moses actually wrote the Pentateuch. His *Tractatus Theologico-Politicus* (1670) presented a rationalist critique of revealed religion and is the founding document of Jewish biblical criticism. The work justifies intellectual and religious freedom, as well as Spinoza's political theories. It was banned by both Jews and Christians. In his *Ethics*, he denies that God has a personality, history or purpose. God, he claims, just is, co-substantial with natural reality, and everything in the world is an aspect of God (pantheism).

Synagogue Synagogues most likely came into being among the exiled Jews in Babylon as a substitute for the lost temple in that middle of the first millennium BCE. The synagogue's crucial difference from the temple is that it never offered sacrifices, but was a place of learning and prayer. As Jewry scattered over the Diaspora, the synagogue became the center of every Jewish community, both physically, as a meeting place, a source of welfare (loans, care of the sick, sleeping accommodation for strangers) and communal administration (through the rabbi and local notables), and spiritually, as the chief locus of the national historical tradition and culture. Today, the Reform Movement in North America uses the word "temple" rather than "synagogue."

Talmud In the two to three centuries following the written version of the Mishna early in the third century CE, its study and development were concentrated in two centers, the Land of Israel and the Babylonian Diaspora. The written compilation and codification of this period of discussion and elaboration of the Mishna is called the Talmud: the version produced in the Land of Israel is called the Jerusalem Talmud, and the other the Babylonian Talmud, which came to command the greater authority. The paramount source of *Halakha* and Jewish spiritual activity in religious circles, the Talmud became the main, even the exclusive, subject of study in Orthodox yeshivas.

T-Y-K-U A Talmudic formula used to signify that, without an agreed solution to a problem, the problem will have to "stand" (in Hebrew: *tyku*, a variant of *tykum* = "let it stand"). In folk etymology, however, the four letters are the initial letters of the phrase *Tishbi yetaretz kushiyot uve'ayot* (Elijah the Tishbite will resolve difficult questions and problems, i.e., the solution must await the return of Elijah the Prophet, the herald of the Messiah).

Vilna Gaon (1720–97): Elijah ben Solomon Zalman, one of the greatest spiritual and intellectual leaders of Jewry in the modern period. He encouraged the Hebrew translation of works on the natural sciences but opposed philosophy and the *Haskalah* (see above), viewing them as threats to faith and tradition. He regarded the slightest attack on any detail of *Halakha* as a blow to the foundations of Torah itself. He violently opposed the practices of Hassidism (see above), and under his leadership Vilna became the center of the *mitnagdim* (opponents) of Hassidism and the long-running battle to repress or contain that movement.

Yahweh or Yahveh The personal name of the God of Israel. By the third century BCE, pronunciation of the name was avoided and *Adonai* (My Lord) substituted. In the early Middle Ages, when the vowel-less biblical text was given vowel signs to ensure correct reading, the four consonants of God's name were given the vowel signs for *Adonai*. Christian scholars pronounced the name "YeHoVaH."

Zealots A religious-political movement of the first century CE which, conceiving of Israel as a theocracy, rejected the idea that the Roman emperor, a mortal being, could be its master. It therefore fought to oust the Romans and restore Jewish sovereignty. It was also apparently willing to use violence against Jews less zealous than they. The Zealots were active in stirring up and leading the Great Revolt of 66 CE. It was a garrison of Zealots who, in 73 CE, committed suicide at Massada, having first killed their women and children, rather than surrender to Roman captivity.

Zedekiah Last king of Judea (597–587 BCE), the king who, refusing the prophet Jeremiah's advice to submit to the Babylonians, brought about the destruction of the First Temple and all of Jerusalem and the exile of the elite of Judah's population to Babylonia in 587 BCE. (See *Jeremiah, Nebuchadnezzar.*)

Zionism Zion as a synonym for Jerusalem goes back to the Second Temple period, when it was used in the psalms to express the yearning of the Jewish people for its homeland. The modern term, Zionism, first appeared at the end of the nineteenth century, designating the political movement for the liberation of the Jewish people through their return to the Land of Israel. Theodore Herzl's *The State of the Jews* and the first Zionist World Congress formed the basis for the movement that established the State of Israel in 1948, thereby creating a country open to all Jews who needed or wanted to live in it.

Zohar The central work in the literature of *Kabbalah,* composed by the Spanish Kabbalist, Moses de Leon, in the last two decades of the thirteenth century. In later centuries, Sabbatean and other circles accorded the work a reverence and status on a par with the Talmud.

INDEX

INDEX

INDEX